PROMOTER AIN'T A DIRTY WORD

PROMOTER AIN'T A DIRTY WORD

HARRY GLICKMAN
General Manager
Portland Trail Blazers

Timber Press
Forest Grove, Oregon

PROMOTER AIN'T A DIRTY WORD
HARRY GLICKMAN

© Copyright 1978 by Timber Press
                    P.O. Box 92, Forest Grove, Oregon 97116

Library of Congress Cataloging in Publication Data

Glickman, Harry
  Promoter ain't a dirty word.

    1. Glickman, Harry. 2. Promoters—United
States—Biography. 3. Sports—Organization and
administration—United States. 4. Public
relations—Sports. I. Title.
GV719.G56A36   796'.092'4[B]   78-5604
ISBN 0-917304-35-7

PRINTED IN THE UNITED STATES OF AMERICA

Cover and book design by Charles S. Politz/Design Council, Inc.

This book, with my sincere love and affection,
is dedicated to:
My mother, Mrs. Bessie Kaplan
My wife, Joanne
My daughter, Lynn Carol Mahaffy
My son, Marshall Jordan Glickman
My daughter, Jennifer Ann Glickman

ACKNOWLEDGEMENTS

I'VE enjoyed writing this book, even if only for my own satisfaction. However, it would never have been published without, first, the agreement to do so and then the constant advice and encouragement of Dick Abel of Timber Press. He has my gratitude.

John White, Publicity Director for the Portland Trail Blazers, can do more with a routine set of statistics than any man I know. His help with research and material has been invaluable and he has my heartfelt thanks.

My secretary, Sandy Sedillo, spent countless hours nights and weekends typing and re-typing the manuscript. She has my sincere thanks well beyond the call of duty.

Others on our staff were most helpful. My thanks to Mrs. Edith Salkeld, George Rickles and Berlyn Hodges in particular.

Finally, without the support of thousands of fans who attended the sports events I describe here, there would have been no reason to attempt this book. They, too, have my sincere gratitude.

TABLE OF CONTENTS

FOREWORD

By Don McLeod
Executive Sports Editor,
The Oregonian (Retired)

THERE'S nothing fictional about *Promoter Ain't a Dirty Word*.

It's a true account of a man's climb to eminence as a sports entrepreneur and no one is more qualified to tell the story than the author, Harry Glickman.

A Portland native, Glickman started modestly as a publicity man for Tex Salkeld, a promoter of the old school, then continued his apprenticeship under the wise tutoring of the legendary Jack Hurley.

After this schooling, Glickman launched his own career as a promoter and his first venture, a professional football game in Multnomah Stadium, was a rousing success.

Since then, he has touched many bases in his chosen field. He brought hockey back to Portland, capping his first season with a championship team, and later dipped into big-time boxing with help from Hurley.

These ventures were successful, but the enterprising promoter really hit the jackpot when he became a leading figure in the Portland Trail Blazers family.

Unlike professional football and hockey, the Blazers weren't an overnight success. In fact, they were woefully weak in the early years, but Glickman, as he relates in his book, employed all his skill as a promoter to keep fan interest alive.

How the Blazers justified his faith, and that of their loyal followers, is entertainingly described in the book.

Before Blazermania, Glickman labored overtime trying to sell the sport and the team, but now, with the National Basketball Association pennant decorating his office wall, he lives the dream of all promoters—an advance sellout for every game.

INTRODUCTION

A sports entrepreneur named Jack Kent Cooke once offered me a job. Jack had just acquired a franchise in the National Hockey League and was planning to build a new arena to house his hockey and basketball teams which, with his penchant for modesty, he was to call the Fabulous Forum.

(The most fabulous thing that ever happened there, as far as I'm concerned, was last May when my Portland Trail Blazers beat his Los Angeles Lakers twice in the opening games of the Western Conference finals en route to four straight wins over the Lakers and, ultimately, the National Basketball Association Championship.)

Because I had enjoyed some success operating the Portland Buckaroos in the Western Hockey League, Cooke apparently thought I'd be a good candidate for general manager of his new hockey team.

"I'm not really a general manager in the sense you mean," I told Cooke, "you'd better get someone else."

"Okay, then maybe you can be the manager of the new building."

"No. I'm not a building manager either."

"I've checked you out with eight people and they all gave you a big recommendation. Just what the hell do you do?"

I was reminded of what the late, great Jack Hurley had once told me prior to a fight we were promoting. "We've got two choices if we want this to be a full house. Either we hustle the tickets and sell 'em or we hire twenty painters to paing some asses on all those seats to make it look like a full house. With the price of painters these days, it's better to sell the tickets."

"My job is to sell tickets," I told Cooke. "I'm a promoter—and I don't think it's a dirty word."

I've spent most of my lifetime hustling tickets to sports events. Along the way I've operated teams which have won championships to two sports in two leagues, climaxed last year when the Trail Blazers won the NBA championship and a city literally went berserk with joy.

This book has been written to tell the story of how major-league sports look from the perspective of the promoter, owner and operator and, in particular, how professional sports look from the perspective of a specific time and place. I hope that it will give sports fans a better understanding of the games they watch and, I hope, enjoy.

PROMOTERS AREN'T BORN

CHAPTER I

IF you accept the premise that the twenty-two teams in the
National Basketball Association, twenty-six teams in major
league baseball, twenty-eight in the National Football League,
and eighteen teams in the National Hockey League comprise
the major leagues of professional sports, and that each of these
teams has an employee known as a General Manager, then I
am fortunate enough to hold one of only ninety-four General
Managers' jobs in all of major league professional sports. If you
contend that the World Hockey Association, the North
American Soccer League and World Team Tennis are also involved in major league sports, I won't argue the point. Considering the fact that people have spent a lifetime in this
business and have never known what Jim McKay described on
Wide World of Sports as "the thrill of victory"—that is, winning a Super Bowl, a World Series, the Stanley Cup or the
NBA Championship—then I consider myself fortunate indeed. My Portland Buckaroos won the Lester Patrick Cup three
times and the Portland Trail Blazers won the NBA championship last spring.

Although I cannot remember a time when I was not ab-
sorbed with sports, there is nothing in my background to indicate that someday I would be involved as a means of earning
a living. I was born in Portland, Oregon, the only son of im-
migrant parents. My father, Sam, was the eldest of eight
children and emigrated from Russia to the United States in the
early 1900's. My mother came to this country after World War
I. The remainder of her family remained behind in Poland and
were later exterminated at Treblinka.

Ballgames and fights were completely alien to my family, who never encouraged me to participate in sports. Like most children of Jewish parents, when we did play ball we were always admonished not to get hurt. If one of us ever did, the injury was slight compared to the licking we received when we got home.

My parents were divorced when I was five years old and I spent the next three years alternating between living with my mother and my grandparents.

If heredity didn't point me to sports, my environment did. When I started attending Shattuck School in the fourth grade my pals, most of whom are still my closest friends today, were all sports nuts. No group of kids anywhere had more fun than we did in South Portland. In the fall we played touch football in the streets or tackle in the parks, and you should see some of the trees which ran interference for us! In the summer we played baseball and later switched to softball. But our real game was basketball, which we started playing at the Jewish Community Center. There, an athletic director named Harry Policar was to have a profound influence on all our lives. We organized a club called the B'nai B'rith Cardinals, which sponsored a basketball team. From 1934 to 1939 we didn't lose more than one game a season.

I realized at an early age that my lack of size, speed and general ability were going to prevent me from realizing my ambition to become a big-league ball player. So I turned my attention to the next best thing—being a radio announcer. We were all very poor in those days, and if we could raise a dime for admission to the bleachers, we'd go watch the Portland Beavers in Sunday doubleheaders at old Vaughn Street park. Minor league baseball, as in many cities throughout the country, was the major sport in town. It received practically all the attention from the newspapers, even in winter, and each opening day was a civic occasion. (Unfortunately for baseball, its operators have been promoting under the theory that 1977 is still 1935 and attending ball games is akin to a civic duty. It simply doesn't work that way anymore.)

I used to look at the people in the press box with envy, especially Rollie Truitt, who for many years broadcast the Beaver games. I thought, what an incredible job, getting into the games free. When I later learned radio announcers and sports writers got paid, that settled my ambition. I wanted to become a sports writer.

I attended every sports event which I could wangle my way into. We used to sneak into fights and wrestling matches at the Civic Auditorium, and later I got in free by hustling programs, pop and ice cream. This also got me into Beaver baseball games and football games at Multnomah Stadium. Occasionally, I'd even make a quarter.

In 1937 I started Lincoln High School. During my senior year I was elected editor of the student newspaper. I assigned myself the job of sports editor. You can't imagine what a thrill it was to be admitted to the press box at Multnomah Stadium with a seat on the 50-yard line.

After graduation in June of 1941, I faced a personal crisis. My mother, who had struggled to raise me working as a seamstress in the ladies garment trade, decided to remarry and move to Seattle. I wasn't a Seattle fan even in those days. I was determined that I wasn't going to move there and go to the University of Washington. My original plan was to stay out of school for a year and work to earn some money to attend the University of Oregon.

That summer I was a counselor at B'nai B'rith summer camp, where I spent my summers as a youngster, first as a camper and later as a counselor under the direction of Harry Policar. I was frustrated and didn't know what to do. One of my buddies, Ray Veltman, urged me to try to go to the University of Oregon that fall, where he would meet me a year later after getting his grades up. I didn't have any money, but full of resolve, I went home and wrote three letters. One was to Howard Hobson, the basketball coach, another to Joe Weinstein, who owned an Army and Navy store in Eugene, and the other to Buck Buchwach, who was then a student working in the Athletic News Bureau of the University of

Oregon. Hobson, not surprisingly, wrote back that they weren't interested in my services as a basketball player, but Joe offered to provide a job working at his store on Saturdays. Buck had preceded me by three years as editor of the Lincoln Cardinal and had gone on to carve quite a name for himself in journalism at Oregon. He wrote back telling me that he had arrived at Oregon with $13 in his pocket, but had been able to work his way through school. He advised me to give it the same try and offered whatever help he could.

For the rest of the summer I took a job in a wholesale clothing warehouse earning $12.50 a week. By the end of the summer I had accumulated $100, which was enough to pay tuition for the year. For the first time in my life I also owned two suits of clothes, both of which, together with all my other possessions, were burned up in a fraternity house fire two months later.

I enrolled at Oregon and Buck was true to his word. He was the assistant director of the Athletic News Bureau and campus correspondent for the Oregon Journal. The plan was that I would inherit his jobs the following year, after he graduated. The director, Bruce Hamby, assigned me stories to rewrite and other odd jobs, which paid $12 a month. I also got a job washing dishes in my fraternity house, Sigma Alpha Mu, which partly paid for room and board. These, together with the job at Joe's store on Saturdays, paid my way the first year.

One of my great thrills that year was working my first football game in the press box at old Hayward Field, sitting alongside L.H. Gregory, Sports Editor of The Oregonian.

Greg was a legend, both in sports and journalism. It's a shame no one wrote a book about Greg before his death a couple of years ago. He was every bit as much a character as any athlete or sport celebrity he ever wrote about.

Greg, in his gruff way, was kind to me then and even kinder when I later became a press agent and promoter. His daily column, "Greg's Gossip," was extremely important to any sports promotion. Never a rapper or knocker, Greg wasn't patronizing, either. If he didn't like something or someone, he would give them the most effective treatment of all—he ignored them.

He had a million idiosyncrasies. In a Chinese restaurant—and he was in one practically every night—he tipped when he sat down, not after the meal. His pockets usually bulged with silver dollars because he hated paper money. He covered sports events by traveling vast distances, preferably by train, for he had a lifetime fondness for railroads. Never in his more than eighty years did Greg ever step inside an airplane. He was a baseball nut and envisioned himself quite a pitcher. I can name a dozen people who claim they accompanied him on a ride from Portland to Pendleton, a distance of about 200 miles, simply to eat a bowl of chili. He liked the way a restaurant there made it.

When Greg came to Eugene to cover a game, I'd sit alongside pounding out a "play-by-play" for the early editions. It was an education in itself.

During spring term, as we were covering a track meet, I noticed Bruce Hamby talking to my friend Buck and Dick Strite, the sports editor of the Eugene Register-Guard. They were whispering, and every once in awhile looked at me. Finally, Bruce came over to say that he was leaving his job as director of the Athletic News Bureau to go with The Oregonian and asked if I was interested in taking over that spring as correspondent for the Oregonian and International News Service. He also promised that I could have both jobs the following fall.

World War II started that winter and most sports programs had to be curtailed or drastically reduced, so the following year, as a green, 18-year-old sophomore, I became the Director of the Athletic News Bureau at the University of Oregon. I was paid $50 a month by the University and earned another $50 from the Oregonian, United Press and International News Service. That was a lot of dough in the fall of 1942, but we all lived it up because we knew we were going into the service.

I joined the Enlisted Reserve Corps and was called into the army in April of 1943. I returned home in March of 1946, in time for the spring term at Oregon, and for the first time in my life I didn't have any kind of job but got through on the GI bill.

That summer fate intervened, as it so often has for me, and I met a person who was to be instrumental in my future sports activities.

I went to the Oregonian one day to ask Greg if I could have my old job back as campus sports correspondent. He introduced me to Don McLeod, who had been appointed Executive Sports Editor, told him I was interested in getting my job back and asked if there was any reason I couldn't have it. McLeod replied, "I'll raise a lot of hell if he doesn't." We have been friends ever since.

Don is a burglar when it comes to beating the opposition to stories. The following year there were many big sports stories at Oregon; the University of Oregon modernized its Athletic Department by placing it under an Athletic Director instead of working through the unwieldy Athletic Board with a Graduate Manager in charge. Tex Oliver resigned as football coach and Jim Aiken succeeded him; the Athletic Board resigned and a new Athletic Director was appointed. It so happened that my boss on the alumni magazine I edited was Les Anderson, a member of the Athletic Board, so I had a good pipeline and got the scoop on all of those stories. That impressed McLeod.

It is a matter of personal pride that I was the first person to mention the name of Norm Van Brocklin to Aiken, the new coach, when he arrived in Eugene. My correspondent's job necessitated attending occasional football practices. Under Tex Oliver, Van Brocklin was a sixth-string tailback in a single-wing offense. His services weren't even needed for scrimmage fodder, so Van would grab a bag of balls, go to the other end of the field, toss one thirty yards, then throw another and hit the first one. I watched him do this countless times. It didn't take a genius to figure out he could throw a football. It only took a Phi Beta Kappa such as Oliver to insist on retaining the single-wing. Van never was noted for his speed afoot and I believe it was he who later coined the phrase, "I run only from fear." But he sure as hell could throw a football.

The first thing Aiken said when we were introduced at a press dinner was, "We're going to use the T-formation, and we've got to find a quarterback who can pass the ball. Are there any around here?" I volunteered Van's name. One session in spring practice convinced Aiken.

Jim rented a home next door to our fraternity house, and he and Van spent countless hours on the living room floor, Mrs. Aiken's best china serving as the two opposing teams. It became popular to write "Dick Miller coaches the line, Frank Zazula coaches the backs and Aiken coaches Van Brocklin." The next year Jim turned the football program around with a 7-3 record and the following year, 1948, the Ducks tied for the Pacific Coast Conference Championship with California. Politics kept them out of the Rose Bowl so they went to the Cotton Bowl instead.

That winter McLeod asked me to go to work for the Oregonian during summer vacation. I had recently committed myself to a job with the Oregon Federation, which involved traveling around the state talking to high-school students about enrolling at the University, so I wasn't able to take the offer. He then asked, "When do you graduate?"

"Next December," I replied.

He said, "Don't make any other plans because you're going to go to work for us as soon as you're through." Since it had been my heart's desire to work for the sports department at the Oregonian, I was thrilled with the prospect.

But fate intervened once again.

At the time the law required a company to give a returning war veteran his former job. The Oregonian had a reporter, Pat Frizzell, who came home that very week and they had to give him the job. McLeod told me to take a couple of publicity accounts to keep going until the next opening on the staff, and volunteered to help me obtain them. So I became a press agent and Don got me my first three accounts.

He arranged for me to get in touch with Tex Salkeld, the boxing promoter in Portland, who needed some help with publicity. I was a fight fan from way back, having sneaked into the Auditorium or sold programs there many times. I used to skip school occasionally to go to the Whitehouse gym to watch fighters train, and when I was carrying newspapers, I used to watch the fighters work out on Saturdays between delivering the daily paper in the morning and the Sunday paper in the afternoon. So becoming a press agent for a fight promoter had a lot of appeal.

The first fight I publicized was between Joe Kahut and Bobby Zander of Los Angeles on March 2, 1948. Kahut had become a local favorite during the war before he went into the Navy; then he was injured in a tractor accident at his farm in Woodburn. This was to be his comeback fight, his first in almost two years. We turned away more people at the Auditorium than we let in that night. There was a mob of some four thousand fans out in the streets trying to buy a ticket. So my first venture in a promotion was a complete sellout and a financial success.

I can't say the same for its artistic success, however, for to be very charitable, you would have to say Zander did not try very hard. Kahut knocked him out in five rounds. It was a real stinker! The next day I confronted Tex and said I was concerned about getting involved in boxing if these were the kind of fights he was going to promote. He explained that he had had the foresight to warn the newspaper men that he feared Kahut's handlers might be "putting one under him." He assured me that he promoted on the level and was going to see to it that nothing like it happened again. He believed in bringing a boxer along slowly against successively better opponents; if he lost occasionally in a good fight, it didn't hurt his drawing ability. I never had occasion to question any other fight he promoted.

That fight started a relationship with one of the greatest characters I have ever known. Salkeld went anywhere from 300 to 350 pounds. He was a rough, tough guy, misnamed Tex as he was originally from California. He had knocked around the boxing game all his life as trainer, manager and promoter. He was an accomplished chef and taught himself to do needlepoint. He put a piano into his duplex as a piece of furniture and literally taught himself how to play it!

Tex's problem was that he was his own worst enemy. When things were tough, he would scratch and hack and do a great job of promoting. When things were going well, he couldn't stand prosperity. We had some good fights and good fighters, but more losing shows than profitable ones.

I was fascinated by the managers in boxing, such as Jack "Doc" Kearns, who had managed Dempsey in his heyday, Tommy Farmer and Gus Wilson from Los Angeles, Joe Herman and Billy Newman from San Francisco, Joe Waterman, Tom Walsh from Chicago, Jake Mintz and Tom Tannas from Pittsburgh, Charlie Goldman (who was Marciano's trainer) and all the other assorted characters who used to come to Portland with their fighters. I could sit for hours and listen to the tales they told. I submit that they represented the last stronghold of rugged individualism in this country. They were tough and shrewd but they had one common characteristic—they were honest. You lived by your word and your handshake. Contracts were for landlords, lawyers and commissions. I've tried to live by the same code in all my dealings as a promoter.

The most incredible character of all, and a guy who was to influence me in promoting more than any other, was the veteran Jack Hurley, whose early claim to fame had been as manager of the Fargo Express, Billy Petrolle. Hurley and two associates, Irving Schoenwald and Jack Begun, had been promoting fights in the Chicago Stadium and hadn't had a losing show in seven years. When the International Boxing Club took over boxing following the reign of Joe Louis as heavyweight champion, they dismissed Schoenwald and Begun but offered to keep Hurley on without his two partners. Hurley wouldn't stand still for it and quit.

When I say the IBC took over boxing, I mean they made it a monopoly such as sports has never seen. They edged their way into the picture by obtaining contracts to conduct an elimination tournament for a successor to Joe Louis as heavyweight champion. Controlling the heavyweight title means having the upper hand in all of boxing, so eventually the IBC owned every championship in every division in the game. It helped, of course, that they also owned the major boxing arenas— Madison Square Garden in New York, the Chicago Stadium, the Olympia in Detroit and the Arena in St. Louis. Most of their title fights were held in their own buildings, but occasionally they would offer a fight to a promoter in some other part of the country as a joint venture.

The president of the IBC was a sportsman named Jim Norris; his partner was Arthur Wirtz. They were also involved with race tracks, and owned the Chicago Blackhawks of the National Hockey League. I was to connect with Wirtz and the Blackhawks in later years.

After refusing to work for the IBC, Hurley took over the contract of a fighter from the Northwest named Harry "Kid" Matthews, who had a great record for winning fights and a lousy record for drawing people. In boxing parlance, he stunk the joint out. Hurley came to Seattle, Matthews' home town, where he had matched him for a fight. He intended to stay ten days; he remained until he died fifteen years later.

Tex brought Matthews to Portland for his first appearance against a fighter named Anton Raadik, from Estonia via Chicago. I happened to be in Seattle and called Hurley in his room at the Olympic Hotel to get some photos of Matthews. It was noon on a Sunday. Hurley said he had already mailed them off to me and said, "Harry, when you call again, please don't call so early in the morning." It was then I learned Hurley's working hours. Like many boxing managers, his day started at noon and continued until dawn, a schedule I pretty much conformed to myself in my press agent days.

I was fascinated with Hurley and we became close friends. I went to Seattle often in those days, as my mother lived there, and spent a lot of time with Jack. There was a great restaurant in Seattle called Von's, which was open all night and had a large menu of excellent food. I doubt if there were ever two nights in a row when I was in Seattle that we wouldn't meet for what was called "the early shift at Von's." That was the big meal at midnight. The late shift was at 3 a.m. before calling it a day, "because if you don't eat something, how will you have the strength to get out of bed?" I would listen to him talk fights and promotions until the wee hours of the morning.

In about this order, Hurley hated food from a freezer, southpaw fighters, women and boxing commissions. But he reserved his most passionate hatred for amateurs. To his way of thinking, the most contemptible name he could call a person was "amateur," and by amateur he meant everyone from a green fighter to a waitress serving her first meal.

Hurley was known by three nicknames—"Professor," "Deacon," and the "Lifetaker." I gave him the name "Professor" after I posed him for a picture with Matthews wearing a cap and gown. It received national exposure. He received the name "Deacon" from Royal Brougham, sports editor of the Seattle P-I, who wrote, "Jack Hurley looks like the stern Deacon in the Presbyterian Church, passing out the collection plate." The monicker "Lifetaker" was given to him by Ray Arcel, the noted boxing trainer. I first heard it when Ray came to Portland with Ezzard Charles.

"How's the Lifetaker?" he asked.

"Who are you talking about?" I asked in return.

"Hurley," he replied.

"Why do you call him that?"

"Because he killed a guy in Chicago once," said Arcel.

Hurley hung around some tough characters in his time in Chicago, but I couldn't believe he had ever killed anyone. "I don't understand what you're talking about," I told Ray.

He explained that during the depression, when Hurley was managing Petrolle, he was one of the few managers in boxing holding any money. At the time, Hurley had an operation for ulcers and was required to eat lightly every three hours. Since he didn't like to eat alone, he took a portly friend along. Passing up a free meal in the depression was like throwing money away; eventually, he ate the guy out of his clothes and had to buy him a new suit; and, eventually, he ate the guy right into the grave.

Although they were later divorced, Hurley was married to a Jewish woman. She taught him how to speak Yiddish well enough so that his Chicago partners never knew he understood when they were talking behind his back. (They were separated at the time and he was living in Seattle while she lived in Chicago.) I was still a bachelor and Hurley was constantly needling me about getting married.

"It's time you signed the papers," he would say. "It's every man's duty to take a gentle little creature and make her happy. Besides," he continued, "you've been getting away with murder long enough."

When Joanne and I became engaged in 1958, we went to Seattle to break the news to my mother. Then we proceeded to Von's, so I could introduce my fiancee to the Deacon. On our way to the restaurant, I said to Joanne, "When I tell him we're engaged, he'll look at me and say 'it's about time—you've been getting away with murder long enough.' "

Jack joined us at a table and ordered a beer. "You'd better have something a little stronger than that," I told him. "It's not every day I celebrate my engagement."

Without batting an eye, Jack looked at Joanne and said "It's about time—he's been getting away with murder long enough."

Joanne almost fell out of her chair.

It was during this period that television was having its first impact on boxing. The IBC had contracts with the networks for a series of fights on Wednesday and Friday nights. Remember the Pabst Blue Ribbon fights on Wednesdays and the Gillette Cavalcade of Sports on Fridays? The IBC had a tidy little deal going for itself. The contracts with the networks and sponsors gave them something in excess of $20,000 a show. Of this amount, they gave the main event fighters $4,000 apiece. In other words, they retained most of the money simply for providing the use of the hall.

That's Glickman and Jack Hurley. The perplexed expression on
Hurley's face is because the boxing manager is trying on a hockey
jersey.

It was said at the time that television had created 30 million new fight fans. What was not said is that the combination of the IBC and network television destroyed a million cash customers. To a promoter, the latter are far more important than the former. Even the most rabid fan was sated with boxing, watching it free on television twice a week. The fighters became nameless. It was a case of "white trunks vs. black trunks."

To prove it, I once bet a sports writer that not half the people in a tavern could name the winner of a fight. One Wednesday I took him to ten taverns and asked each bartender who had won the fight. In seven out of ten the answer was "black trunks." Helluva name for a fighter. For instance, Ralph "Tiger" Jones appeared on television something like 52 times. You gonna tell me there was that much demand for his services? But he never got knocked out or knocked anyone else out, so the sponsors got in all their commercials.

I stood by and watched television literally destroy boxing. It shaped my attitude about television in every other sport with which I was to get involved.

I will always rate the job Hurley did building up Matthews from an overgrown middleweight to a contender for the heavyweight championship of the world as one of the greatest promotions in the history of sports. Hurley fought the IBC every step of the way. In fact, he helped bring about a congressional investigation of that outfit, which was later convicted of conspiracy to monopolize boxing and was ordered, among other things, to divest itself of its interest in Madison Square Garden.

Hurley literally forced a match between Matthews and Rocky Marciano, the winner to fight Joe Walcott for the heavyweight title. On one of his trips East, Hurley had gone to Philadelphia to watch Marciano fight Lee Savold, a washed-up former heavyweight contender. Marciano won the fight, but Savold made him look terrible and Hurley was convinced that his man Matthews would easily defeat Marciano. After a lot of maneuvering, the fight was scheduled in Yankee Stadium in New York in July of 1952.

Hurley was not only confident of defeating Marciano, he had a commitment for a title fight with Walcott and even had an "arrangement" for Matthews' first defense of his heavyweight championship, against Cesar Brion of Argentina. On a trip to Washington stirring up publicity for Matthews with his opposition to the IBC, Hurley was approached by a gentleman who represented himself as a member of the Argentine Embassy in Washington. He said that if Hurley's fighter were to win the heavyweight championship, he was prepared to make a lucrative offer on behalf of an Argentine syndicate for Matthews to defend the title in Argentina against Brion, a rated fighter at that time. Included in the offer, aside from the normal purse to the champion, was a satchel containing one million dollars in cash, which was to go to Hurley and Matthews. It seems it would have been a feather in Juan Peron's cap for an Argentinian to win the heavyweight championship of the world!

When Hurley related this story to me, I accused him of using Chinese chocolates. Not long afterward, however, Peron was booted out of Argentina; included in his baggage was 20 million dollars in loose cash for spending money. A million dollars to Hurley for a heavyweight title fight would have been peanuts and a worthwhile investment. I can't tell you that this story is true, but I can tell you I believe it.

At any rate, it was to no avail. Marciano knocked Matthews out with a left hook to the chin in the second round and ruined Hurley's dreams of managing the heavyweight champion. It would have been better had Hurley never gone to Philadelphia to see the Marciano-Savold fight. Savold was all through but he was a crafty veteran who made Marciano look awkward and clumsy.

So convinced was Hurley that his fighter would win that he violated one of his own cardinal rules—he made a bet on Matthews. A friend of his in New York, Sammy Richman, had begged him not to bet on the fight. He said, "Jack, if Matthews wins the right, the ten grand you win will be peanuts, because you'll wind up making a million dollars with a heavyweight champion. If you're going to bet, at least bet the other way, so in case Matthews loses, you'll have an extra ten grand in your kick." Hurley wouldn't listen to him.

After Matthews' first appearance, the Raadik fight in 1950, Hurley's man boxed nine more times in Portland with Tex Salkeld promoting, and drew a capacity house every time. But Tex started getting into needless arguments with Hurley. I could see that a split between the two was inevitable.

After each Matthews fight in Portland, Tex would immediately ask Hurley for another date. Hurley would reply, "Tex, the fans are going to get tired of him fighting these bums. Let's take our time and see if we can dig up a more respectable opponent."

Salkeld always had a surefire answer. "I'm not getting tired of these paydays, are you?"

"No, of course not," Hurley would answer, "but sooner or later these fans are going to revolt. Let's wait until a good opponent appears."

In December of 1951, Hurley accepted a guarantee of $25,000 from Larry Atkins, the promoter in Cleveland, for Matthews to fight Danny Nardico in the annual Christmas benefit card there. It turned out to be a great fight with Matthews winning a unanimous decision. A rematch looked like an excellent attraction.

Salkeld kept pressing Hurley to hold the rematch in Portland, but Hurley insisted he would put the fight in Boise in an outdoor stadium the following summer. (Matthews was originally from Boise and was a good attraction there for two outdoor cards in the summer months.) Salkeld would insist, "But I can draw more money than they can in Boise."

Hurley would reply, "I know that, but I can make more money with the fight in Boise."

"I don't know what your deal is in Boise, but I will give you the same deal in Portland," Salkeld answered.

Hurley said, "My deal in Boise is that we get our normal 30% of the gate, but we also split the profits with Tex Hager, the promoter."

"In that case," said Salkeld, "you've got the same deal in Portland."

I told Tex, "You're crazy to offer Hurley half the profits of the show. He isn't entitled to them. Let him take the Nardico fight to Boise; there will be other fights for Portland."

The Nardico rematch never came off, but the offer had repercussions. Hurley thought the offer was for all future Portland fights. Salkeld insisted it was for the Nardico match only. Any surprise a schism developed between them?

I wasn't paid very much for my work as press agent for Tex. We had no specific arrangement and I didn't draw a salary. After each show I would be paid, sometimes as little as $25, sometimes as much as $200, but I wasn't earning much of a living. Fortunately, I had a couple of other publicity accounts to keep me going. I handled publicity for the annual Shriner's Hospital All-Star football game and did publicity and wrote the chart for Multnomah Kennel Club dog racing during the summer. But at no time in my five years as a press agent did my income exceed $5,000.

Each time Tex would run a promotion and make some money on a Matthews fight, he would blow it back trying to build up another fighter. He borrowed money all over town and was stuck about $10,000. He kept telling me if he ever got even he would give me a piece of the action.

The big fight everyone wanted at that time was between Matthews and Rex Layne of Utah, a leading contender for the heavyweight championship. Every promoter around was getting into the act, trying to make that fight for Seattle, or Las Vegas, or Boise, or Salt Lake, or, of course, Portland.

By that time we had started running some of the bigger shows at the Pacific International Livestock Exposition in Portland. For instance, we brought Ezzard Charles out to box Kahut, the winner of the first fight I had publicized, in December of 1951 shortly after Charles lost the heavyweight championship of the world. He stopped Kahut in the fifth round. It was an old barn of a building but it did have 10,000 seats. Small capacities have plagued me ever since I became a press agent and promoter.

One weekend Hurley was in Portland while Matthews finished training for a fight. We were both in our cups a bit when Hurley unloaded and said he was tired of the aggravation he was having with Salkeld. "From now on," he said, "you're going to be the promoter in Portland."

I told Jack I appreciated the proposition, but I had a sense of loyalty to Tex and wanted to see him come out even. "Jack, if you would give him the Rex Layne fight in Portland, it would get him even, and after that I would have no qualms about leaving. But I'd like to see him pay off his markers."

Principals in the fight between Harry Matthews and Rex Lane held at the P-I Building in Portland in 1952. From left, Jack Hurley, Harry Matthews, Rex Lane and Marve Jenson, Lane's manager.

Without undue modesty, I would have to say I was responsible for making the Layne-Matthews fight for Portland. We held it at the P-I building in May of 1952. It attracted a record crowd of more than 10,000 and a record gross gate of $66,000. It also caused the fire marshall to lock the building the next day. Matthews won the decision, which earned him the Marciano fight.

Tex got even, Hurley got the Marciano fight and Tex and I got divorced.

For a time, our personal relationship deteriorated, but I'll always be glad we became good friends again before his death. His widow, Edith, worked in our ticket department for many years prior to her recent retirement.

When I left Tex in the spring of 1952, I told him I had other plans; for by then something had happened to launch my own career as a promoter in another sport.

PROMOTER AIN'T A DIRTY WORD

CHAPTER II

MOST good things have happened to me by accident. In December of 1951 I was spending the holiday season in Los Angeles pursuing a romantic interest. As I do to this day when I travel, I took in as many sports events and met as many sports writers as possible. I had a date to visit Benny Woolbert, Executive Sports Editor of the Herald-Examiner, one evening at his home. He called me that morning to say he had to attend a cocktail party for a short time. I should meet him there; we would have a drink and then proceed to his house. So, I met him at the Sportsman's Rendezvous, which was owned by a boxing manager named Suey Welch and a sports writer named Bob Hunter.

The occasion was a party given by the Los Angeles Rams, who had just won the National Football league championship, for members of the media. I arrived, greeted a few acquaintances and, as so often happens at cocktail parties, was left alone in a corner of the room with a drink in my hand. A gentleman walked over and introduced himself as Harold Pauley, one of the owners of the Rams. We got to talking and I told him that the Rams, having just won the NFL championship, and with Norm Van Brocklin of Oregon as their quarterback, should give consideration to playing one of their pre-season games in Portland.

"That's a real coincidence," said Pauley. "We were going over our pre-season schedule today and one of the places we thought about was Portland. Are you from there?"

"Yes," I replied.

"What do you do?" I told him I was a press agent involved in sports.

"You'd know," he said, "what could we draw up there?"

"All you could put in our stadium," I replied.

"How many does it hold?"

"At that time of the year, about 29,000, because it's also used by the Portland Beavers for baseball games."

"That's very interesting," said Pauley, "let's go over here and talk to Dan." Dan was Dan Reeves, the President of the Rams.

Pauley introduced me to Reeves. He was into the sauce pretty good. "This is Harry Glickman from Portland," said Pauley, "and he's going to put up a big guarantee for us to go up and play there next year."

"I'm not putting up any big guarantee, but what would it take to get you to play one of your pre-season games in Portland?" Reeves replied that it would take $40,000— $20,000 for each team. The opponent he had in mind was the Chicago Cardinals.

"Will you take a percentage?"

"No," replied Reeves, "we'll play for a flat guarantee."

"How soon do you have to know?"

"I'm going to the league meeting in Philadelphia in about ten days and I would like to have our pre-season schedule wrapped up by then."

"Will you give me ten days to try and raise the money?"

"Yes, let me hear from you."

I went back to Portland and talked to everyone I knew who I thought owned $40,000. Guarantees for a flyer on a football game didn't interest anyone of means, and I couldn't raise the dough.

Dan Reeves was one of the finest gentlemen I ever knew in sports. Reeves brought the major leagues to the Pacific Coast, but he is not given the credit he deserves for it. Most people think major league sports in the West came with Walter O'Malley and the Dodgers, but Reeves was there years before, when it was still considered a reckless gamble.

In 1945 the Cleveland Rams, owned by Reeves, won the NFL championship, but he couldn't even attract a decent crowd to the title game. Reeves was determined to move to Los Angeles. It was considered so risky, however, that he wasn't sure that he would get permission from the league to make the switch. He took a lease on the Cotton Bowl in Dallas in case the league wouldn't let him go to Los Angeles.

The league meetings were being held in New York, where Reeves lived. The meetings started early and lasted well into the night, so he didn't see his wife for a week. One morning, over breakfast, she read in the New York Times that the Rams were going to Los Angeles and realized that she would be moving her home!

It was Reeves who first introduced a genuine scouting system to professional football. *Now* everyone knows where Grambling is, but the Rams had Tank Younger before anyone else heard of the place. When they talk about a sportsman in the genuine sense of that word, Dan Reeves was the embodiment of it.

I kept in touch with Reeves and he kept waiting because he thought Portland would be a good place for a Rams game. Finally, I interested a fellow named Dave Horenstein, brother of a former Lincoln High School teammate, in putting up the guarantee. We were also involved in the promotion of the Matthews-Layne fight at the time. I told Dave the fight would draw in excess of $50,000.

"You're crazy, but I'll tell you what," he said, "if that fight draws what you say it will, I'll put up the $40,000 for the football game."

Well, the fight drew more than I said it would and Dave, true to his word, put up the guarantee. So I had my first venture as a promoter.

Dave gave me a check for $40,000. Under my contract with the Rams and Cardinals, the money was to be placed in escrow and paid to them when the game was over. I took the check to my bank and told an officer what I wanted them to do with the money.

He started asking questions like, "What constitutes a football game?"

I said, "Well, these two teams are going to be playing in Portland and the next day the papers will report it. I'll bring over the clippings to prove they played the game. Then you release the money and give them each a check for $20,000."

"No," replied the banker.

I had to hire a lawyer and it cost me $250 to put the $40,000 in escrow.

I never worked harder on anything in my life. I had a small office in the Dekum Building at the time and a telephone answering service. I did hire a secretary who came in three hours three days a week to help with the mail orders, but I did everything else myself. I wrote the publicity, hustled the tickets, made all the arrangements. It was a huge success. We attracted a capacity crowd of 29,122. We didn't have one unsold ticket in Multnomah Stadium, including those behind the posts. It was also a helluva game, the Rams winning 24-14.

Let's get it straight. The game was such a success not because of my promotional brilliance, but because the Rams were the NFL champions and had as their quarterback the finest player we have ever produced in Oregon, my old buddy Norm Van Brocklin. Van to this day ranks as the greatest competitor I have ever known in sports. He was the attraction and he was the reason we had a sellout.

An interesting coincidence occurred at the time of this game. The Rams had just hired a young man as their publicity director. They sent him to Portland on his first trip for the club. His name was Pete Rozelle and he is today, of course, the renowned Commissioner of the National Football League. Pete and I sort of grew up in this business together, and I am one of his strongest boosters and admirers.

We had a small problem with publicity for the football game, however. The Women's National Amateur Golf Championship was being held at Waverly Country Club in Portland the week preceding the game. It was won by a Hawaiian named Jackie Pung. Each day she danced the hula on the 18th green. Stories and pictures saturated the newspapers, relegating our football game to second place. Jackie Pung became a standing joke between Pete and myself. When he became Commissioner of the NFL, I sent him a congratulatory wire, adding the good wishes of Jackie Pung in a toast to the new Czar.

The success of that game was noted throughout the NFL. It was the sparkplug for a series of NFL games in Portland up through 1969, when our stadium could no longer accommodate the crowds necessary to interest the teams in coming to Portland. Teams were once delighted to come to town and take out $25,000 apiece, but pre-season games today gross upwards of half a million dollars. There is no way we can produce that kind of money. But during that interval we scheduled virtually every team in the NFL prior to its expansion and merger with the American Football League. It gave me the opportunity and good fortune to meet such people as Tony and Vic Morabito of the San Francisco 49ers, Art Rooney of the Pittsburgh Steelers, Paul Brown, formerly of the Cleveland Browns and now of the Cincinnati Bengals, Vince Lombardi of the Green Bay Packers, Well Mara of the New York Giants, Tex Schramm of the Dallas Cowboys and many others.

Lombardi became a favorite of mine from the day he first took over as Coach and General Manager of the Packers, long before he was to become the most famous personality in professional football.

I got to know him when in 1959 I was stuck without a game. The Rams and 49ers, one or the other of which were usually scheduled because of their proximity to Portland, both had filled their pre-season schedules. The team I wanted was the Philadelphia Eagles, because they had just made a trade with the Rams to obtain Van Brocklin. But to bring the Eagles to the coast for one game involved a lot of additional transportation expense. I needed an opponent desperately.

Lombardi had just taken over the Packers. I called him as soon as he arrived in Green Bay. The Packers were booked to play the 49ers in San Francisco, so I offered him a second game on the coast. Having been in Portland as an assistant with the Giants, he readily agreed. I explained to Vince that we had always made both teams the same offer, whether they played on a guarantee or a percentage. I wouldn't be able to do so in this case, however, because I would have to bring the Eagles all the way from the East for only one game. Since he was scheduled to play in San Francisco, his "carfare" would be modest. I said I was offering him a guarantee of $17,000 but I wanted him to know up front that I was giving the Eagles an additional $13,000 for travel expenses. He agreed to the arrangement immediately.

In the same conversation, I inquired about rumors that he might be trading for George Shaw, another product of the University of Oregon. It is generally forgotten that Shaw was runner-up for Rookie of the Year when he entered the NFL with the Baltimore Colts. It is no exaggeration to say that had Shaw not been injured in his second year in a game against the Chicago Bears, football fans would probably have never heard of Johnny Unitas. When Unitas took over as quarterback of the Colts and led them to a pair of titles, Shaw became expendable and was traded to the Giants, where Lombardi was an assistant coach.

A game matching Van Brocklin against Shaw was a cinch sellout in Portland. Lombardi said he would very much like to have Shaw but he didn't think the Giants would give him up, and "I don't have anything here to give for him anyway," he said. I called Vince a couple of days later to complete arrangements for the game and again inquired about Shaw. He said he had been in touch with the Giants but that he was unavailable. "Anyway," he said, "I've started to look at the films of last year's games and there's a quarterback here who doesn't look all that bad. His name is Bart Starr." The rest, of course, is history.

Another of my favorite people in the NFL is one of the most respected coaches in the history of the game, Paul Brown. He first brought his Cleveland Browns to Portland in 1960. The team practiced at Pacific University in Forest Grove the follow-

Norm Van Brocklin (right) and promoter Harry Glickman look over Multnomah Stadium prior to the Atlanta Falcons-Philadelphia Eagles National Football League exhibition game in 1960.

ing week, awaiting another game on the coast. Brown invited me to have lunch with him when I brought his check for the game. I arrived at the appointed hour but had to wait. Paul finally appeared, apologizing all over the place for keeping me waiting. He explained that he had just told a player he was letting him go, adding, "No matter how long you're in the business, that is still the toughest job there is to do." This from a man who had the reputation of being a hard-bitten martinet.

I have thought of Brown many times since, when I have had to let players on our hockey and basketball teams go. He was absolutely right—it's the lousiest part of the job.

"The greatest game ever played" is the label tagged onto the NFL title game in 1958 between the New York Giants and Baltimore Colts. It was the first game with sudden-death over-time, according to legend. Not true. The first NFL game with sudden-death overtime was played in Portland between the Los Angeles Rams and New York Giants on August 28, 1955. It was the second game we had that year. After the first one, driving Dan Reeves to the airport, I suggested a couple of rule changes: 1. Indicate penalties on the specific offender and announce it. In other words, if Smith holds, Smith should be called for the infraction. 2. Mark the yardline stripes from "0" to "100" instead of from "0" to "50" and then from "50" to "0." When a guy kicks a punt from the 37-yard line to the other team's 23, the fans have to stop to compute the yardage. On the other hand, if the kick is from the 42 to the 84-yard line, the fans can easily figure out it's a 42-yard punt. I wanted to experiment with both of these rules in a pre-season game. Reeves readily gave his approval and added, "For publicity purposes announce it as a sudden-death overtime, something the league has been talking about for some time."

I got in touch with the Commissioner, Bert Bell. He gave his approval for sudden-death overtime and marking the sidelines, but was vehemently against calling individual infractions. (I am pleased to note that the NFL now does call individual infractions.) Not dreaming it would ever happen, we were using sudden death purely as a publicity stunt. Well, wouldn't you know, the game ended in a 17-17 tie. It seems that the management had neglected to inform the two coaches that they were going to have overtime. An argument ensued on the playing field. I had visions of the teams walking off the field to a chorus of boos, with my head in a wringer. Finally, we got it straightened out. The Rams took the kickoff, marched to a touchdown and won the first sudden-death game in the history of the National Football League.

Portland became the best city outside the NFL for pre-season games. Several of the teams elected to train in Oregon. The New York Giants had their training camp at Willamette University in Salem in 1955 and 1956. Jim Lee Howell was their head coach, but he had a pretty good group of assistants, including men like Tom Landry and Lombardi. I'll never forget a practice session when Lombardi chewed out Frank Gifford, one of the super-stars of the NFL, as if he were a raw rookie. Incidentally, I took Gifford to several radio appearances that year and he told me he was considering a career as an announcer. Today, of course, he is the play-by-play man on Monday Night Football.

With the success of the NFL games in Portland, other promotions became available. In 1952 I began a long association with the Harlem Globetrotters, which continues to this day. I met Abe Saperstein, the owner of the Globetrotters, and told him if he was ever looking for a promoter in Portland, I was available. Abe was one of the most loyal guys ever, and his games in Portland were handled by the Portland Basketball Association, which furnished an opponent during the days when the Globetrotters were getting started. Games were held at the old Portland Ice Arena, but when that building was closed by the fire marshal, Abe assigned me the job of promoting the Globetrotter games. We have never had a scrap of paper between us in all the years I promoted the Globetrotters.

Through a friend in Los Angeles, Arnie Mills, I was able to obtain Liberace for my first venture into something other than sports. It was, of course, an easy sellout, so I started thinking I knew something about the entertainment business. I booked a Northwest tour for Judy Garland, and wound up with exactly eighteen bucks to my name when it was over. We scheduled her into Eugene, Portland, Seattle and Vancouver. Eugene was fair, Portland pretty good with a sellout on the final appearance, Seattle was a disaster when she cancelled out because of alleged illness. Three days later she was to appear in Spokane. Her husband, Sid Luft, asked me to go ahead and arrange all the interviews possible for Judy in an effort to salvage something from the tour. Among other things, I scheduled a press conference in the lobby of the Davenport Hotel the day of the show. Judy didn't appear. I called her room. I heard Luft talking to her in the background. He said he'd call me back. He didn't, so I went up to the room. No answer. I threatened to kick in the door. They finally answered. She was playing poker with some of the dancers in the show. I explained to her that she was due downstairs for interviews. She said it was her day off, she had never been informed and she wasn't coming. I said, "I don't know anything about that, but your husband told me to arrange it, people are waiting downstairs and I want you to come down."

"Tell them to go. . .," she said. I almost dropped my teeth!

This from the little girl who sang "Over the Rainbow"! She didn't appear, either. I have had other offers involving show business promotions, but Judy Garland effectively made me a sports promoter.

But football wasn't my only sport. After Matthews lost to Marciano, Hurley brought him back to the Northwest to revive him. He wanted me to become a promoter in Portland now that Salkeld and I had parted. But Tex still had political influence so I wasn't able to obtain a promoter's license in Portland. I got one in Seattle instead. It's a strange thing, but I have rarely had problems with players, promoters or teams. I've invariably had problems, however, with landlords and Commissions. I think it noteworthy that boxing is the only sport which is controlled by politically appointed Commissions. Its shabby record should tell us something about mixing politics and sports. We need politicians in sports like I need an extra neck.

In 1953 Matthews boxed Freddy Beshore in Portland. Hurley and I were to leave immediately after the fight for Chicago, where the rematch was slated between Marciano and

Walcott. The purpose of the trip was to offer the winner a guarantee of $250,000 to fight Matthews for the title in Seattle. On the plane to Chicago I told Hurley I thought we were wasting our time because we wouldn't be able to get Marciano. His manager, Al Weill, and Hurley were bitter enemies. Anyone connected with the IBC was automatically Hurley's enemy. The fight, incidentally, ended in a quick one-round knockout, causing a Chicago sports writer to comment, "the sponsors on television (Gillette) used a lot of their product cutting their own throats over that fiasco."

Matthews had gone to London that winter to box Johnny Williams, the British Empire heavyweight champion, but Matthews came down with a bad back and the fight was cancelled. In the meantime, Don Cockell won the British Empire heavyweight championship. I asked Hurley about the possibilities of obtaining him as an opponent. He said, "He's a big fat guy that doesn't look like a fighter, but he can box like hell. Matthews should beat him but it could be a good fight. Maybe there's a chance we can get him." So we returned to Seattle and arranged a fight with Cockell. The fight broke all attendance and gate receipts records in the Northwest. It grossed $96,606 with a crowd of more than 14,000. The fight was a corking good one and Matthews should have won the decision. But Cockell knocked him down three times in the ninth round and that caused the referee and one judge to give the fight to Cockell, even though I thought Matthews won handily. There was a rematch the following summer and it drew another gate of more than $90,000.

Meanwhile, I was continuing my annual promotion of NFL pre-season games, the Harlem Globetrotters, and dabbled around in a few other sports ventures. In 1954, a writer on the Oregon Journal, Tom Humphrey, led an editorial campaign, "Sad Sack City or Major League Town?" Included was a proposal for a new coliseum. It passed in an election in 1954.

I had been promoting other people's attractions for a long time. I was now determined to see what I could do with one of my own. It took six years from the time the levy was approved in 1954 to build Memorial Coliseum. In 1960, when it was completed, I was ready with my own professional sports franchise, the Portland Buckaroos of the Western Hockey League.

THE FAIRY TALE BUCKAROOS

CHAPTER III

CANDOR compels me to disclose that my preference for the Portland franchise was a National Basketball Association team.

Starting in 1954, I carried on a continuing, voluminous and—as it turned out—worthless correspondence with the then Commissioner of the NBA, Maurice Podoloff.

In 1957 and 1958 I promoted two post-season NBA All-Star games, both to show my own interest and to demonstrate that Portland would support major league basketball. The first was a game between the Boston Celtics, as usual fresh from winning another championship, and a group of NBA All-Stars. The second was a game between the East and West All-Stars.

Since there was no building in Portland large enough to hold the games, we promoted them at the Hudson Bay High School gym in Vancouver, Washington. It had a capacity of about 3,800 seats. I also promoted games each year at the Civic Auditorium in Seattle.

I approached Bill Sharman, who was nearing the end of his career with the Celtics, about a coaching position. We agreed to talk if I had any luck in obtaining a franchise. This didn't happen, of course, and Sharman later went on to coach championship teams in three different leagues—the old ABL founded by Abe Saperstein, the American Basketball Association and, finally, the NBA with the Los Angeles Lakers.

I even undertook to promote an NBA league game, bringing the Minneapolis Lakers and Cincinnati Royals to Portland on February 12, 1959, for a game at the old P-I building. I knew going in that the best I could do was to break even and that is exactly what happened. But we did attract a crowd of 4,996 in a further effort to prove that Portland was ready for a team of its own.

I was finally convinced I didn't stand a chance after a meeting with Podoloff in New York. At the time, both the NBA and the Harlem Globetrotters had offices in the Empire State Building. The Globetrotters' office, incidentally, was operated by Walter Kennedy, who was destined to succeed Podoloff as Commissioner and to expand the league. I had lunch with Abe Saperstein and then met with Podoloff. Trying to impress him with the fact that we could draw out West, I said, "I just left a guy who knows all about basketball all over this country and all over the world. He certainly knows the Northwest. Don't take my word for it; check it out with him."

"Who?" asked Podoloff.

"Abe Saperstein," I replied.

"Hold on a minute," said the diminutive Commissioner. "Abe Saperstein would get on an airplane to London faster than I would take the subway to Brooklyn."

I knew then and there I was licked.

Meanwhile, I began delving into the possibility of a franchise in the Western Hockey League. On a visit to Seattle one day I called Al Leader, the president of the league, to inquire about interest in Portland.

He was not only cordial, he was downright enthusiastic about the possibility of Portland returning to the WHL, and of my involvement in the operation.

"We are certainly planning on returning to Portland when the new building is ready," Leader told me. "We have a franchise in New Westminster playing in an old building and we have been saving Portland for the operator of that franchise. His name is Fred Hume."

"Would he be interested in selling his franchise?" I asked Al.

"He might be if you would be interested in buying it."

"Any idea what the price might be?"

"No, but I'll make some inquiries and if you'd like, I will arrange a meeting with him."

Al set up a meeting immediately following the 1959 season at his offices in Seattle. I went with my attorney and Mr. Hume came accompanied by his coach and General Manager, Hal Laycoe.

Let me make it clear that I didn't look upon a franchise in the Western Hockey League as some sort of consolation prize. On the contrary, I was enthusiastic and excited about the project. At the time, I was also managing Multnomah Stadium in Portland and, as a result, was on the luncheon and dinner circuit. Everywhere I went, there were questions about the new Coliseum and the events to be held there. And everywhere I was asked about the return of hockey to Portland. I concluded that if a fraction of the people who inquired about hockey would attend games, we would have tremendous crowds.

I was a long-time, if casual, hockey fan myself. I had watched the old Portland Buckaroos play in the '30s and one of my sports heroes was their goalkeeper, Airtight Andy Aitkenhead. In my press agent days there was a hockey team in Portland, first named the Penguins and then the Eagles. I rarely missed a Sunday night game.

At the meeting in Seattle Mr. Hume, a former mayor of Vancouver, B.C., indicated he would be interested in selling his franchise. He mentioned a purchase price of $85,000. I had no idea what a franchise in the WHL was worth, but later learned it was a high figure for franchises at that time. The league was going broke in almost every city and had survived primarily because of Leader's tenacity in keeping it together. He knew that, eventually, there would be new buildings in the major Pacific Coast cities capable of attracting big crowds to Western Hockey League games.

I didn't quibble with Mr. Hume and accepted his price. I told him I would need a little time to complete my financing. While it wasn't a condition of the sale, Hume wanted Laycoe to go along as the coach. Leader had also recommended Laycoe, and since I didn't know any other coaches in hockey or how to go about finding one, we had a general understanding that if we brought the team to Portland, Laycoe would come as part of the deal.

When you are involved in sports you get to know people in other facets of the entertainment business. I became acquainted with Al Foreman, who operated a string of theaters. He advised me that if I brought a franchise to Portland, he would be interested in joining and financing the venture. I worked out a deal with Foreman and started looking for other partners. Al wanted to cut in two people who had done him favors in the past. We discussed it with them, but they didn't want a piece of the action, a decision they came to regret.

Al was a good friend of Ted Gamble, who had also been in the theater business and then became involved in a number of other profitable ventures. We met with Gamble, who said yes in five seconds. Ted wanted to include Howard Lane, then General Manager of television station KOIN, which was owned jointly by Gamble and the Newhouse newspaper chain. This sounded like a bonanza for two reasons. First, Gamble had a lot of juice around town and I thought he could be instrumental in working out a lease on the building. I was later to learn otherwise. Also, the fact that he owned a piece of the television station certainly could not hurt our promotion possibilities.

The deal we finally worked out was that Foreman, Lane and Gamble would each take 25% of the action. I was assigned 19% for putting the deal together and my part of the investment was to be paid over a period of years out of my salary. Nothing could have been fairer than that. The other 6% was reserved for a friend of Gamble's, Clay Brown, who had formerly been President of the Portland Beavers baseball team when he and Gamble were involved in that operation.

The deal was structured so that we would put up $25,000 in cash, $6,250 each from Gamble, Lane and Foreman and $1,500 from Brown. My $4,750 was to come out of my salary sometime down the line. The remainder of the purchase price and operating capital were to be borrowed from a bank.

Foreman and I drove to Vancouver to conclude our negotiations with Hume. At dinner we agreed on all the details.

"Fine," we told Hume, "we will have a check for you as soon as we return to Portland."

"One thing," Hume added as an afterthought, "I expect the money in Canadian funds." Since the Canadian dollar was worth 5% more than the U.S., the purchase price was actually $88,500. We didn't quibble about the increased price and closed the deal to purchase the franchise.

Our most immediate problem was what to do with the ten players we had acquired from New Westminster. The Coliseum would not be ready for another year due to a long political hassle initiated by Joe Dobbins, a used car dealer, requiring two city-wide elections to settle. That delayed construction of the building and reduced the seating capacity, because of the inflation of construction costs.

The Victoria Club was just about ready to fold, having experienced a disastrous year the season before. An arrangement was worked out whereby the players from New Westminster would be assigned to Victoria for a year and Laycoe would go there as coach. This deal was completed at a league meeting in Calgary and we shook hands with the representative from Victoria. As far as I was concerned, that was a contract. It turned out that hockey people weren't fight managers and handshakes didn't always mean you lived by your word.

Part of our deal was that we would loan them all of the New Westminster players. The only thing we asked in return was that Victoria permit us to purchase their goalkeeper, Marcel Pelletier, at the end of the season. A purchase price of $2,000 was agreed upon.

Laycoe moved to Victoria to set up the operation and soon found how bad things were. His trainer, Berlyn Hodges, tried to sell program advertising only to discover that there were checks bouncing all over town, with unpaid bills galore. It was a chaotic situation.

When Leader learned of the desperate situation in Victoria, he called an emergency meeting of the league. A fellow named Jim Pigott had been operating a franchise in Saskatoon, but the league had unofficially committed the Los Angeles territory to him when a new sports arena was completed there. Leader prevailed upon Pigott to operate in Victoria the ensuing year. As his representative he sent one of hockey's all-time greats, Frank Boucher, to the meeting. I met with Boucher the night before the meeting to tell him about our deal to loan the players free in return for the right to purchase Pelletier. Boucher said Pigott would not agree to any condition involving Pelletier. I didn't think this was a fair shake and it was contrary to the deal we agreed to in Calgary. If I hadn't relented, however, the league was going to fold Victoria only two weeks prior to the start of the season, disrupting the schedule, among many other things. So I conceded.

It turned out that the meeting in Victoria was one of the most explosive in the history of the league and I, unwittingly, was the cause of it.

When we had made our deal to buy the franchise, Laycoe called to say there was a young player named Gerry Goyer who had performed pretty well for Seattle during the recent playoffs. He said that Seattle would try for Goyer's amateur reinstatement at a price of $750 and we should immediately claim him, as he would be a good prospect for Portland. This is exactly what happened and I put in a claim for Goyer.

Leader called me and explained that Seattle had brought Goyer up during the playoffs with the explicit assurance that he would regain his amateur standing. Leader said Goyer was not interested in playing professionally and he had given the player his word that he would get him his amateur card back, which was permissable under the rules of hockey. He asked me to pass on Goyer and I agreed.

I immediately got a call from Laycoe saying that we should not pass on Goyer. I explained that I had given Mr. Leader my word and I wasn't going to start operating in hockey by breaking it, even though it might be a mistake. I had checked with Laycoe before giving Leader my word, but Laycoe complained he had been under a great deal of pressure and now wanted to change his mind. I said it was too late for that and we were going to pass on Gerry Goyer.

At the meeting in Victoria the issue arose and, to the astonishment of most of the people there, we learned that Leader had been acting in a dual capacity, first as President of the Western Hockey League and secondly as General Manager of the Seattle team.

The Seattle club had previously folded and the league was left without an American city. Several of the Governors of the league had instructed Leader to do everything possible to get Seattle back into operation. Leader approached a group of his friends about investing in the franchise. They had agreed to share the losses on the assumption that they would recoup when Seattle obtained a new building. They committed on the condition that Leader operate the franchise for them.

Al had approached two or three of the Governors and they had agreed that he should act in a dual capacity. Al, a decent and honest guy, made the mistake of not informing the other members of the league, who would probably have consented to the same arrangement. You can imagine the look on the faces of these Governors when they learned that Leader, supposedly a neutral President, had actually been operating the Seattle club. It caused him needless future problems because he was to be constantly and unfairly accused of always favoring Seattle.

Anyhow, it worked out that Pigott took over the franchise with our players assigned to Victoria. It also turned out they had a heck of a year, finishing in second place in their division and going to the finals in the playoffs, eventually losing to Vancouver.

In the spring of 1960, I left the Stadium to open a small office in downtown Portland. My next move turned out to be one of my best. A friend of mine, George Rickles, was then pumping gasoline for his father-in-law. He had at first worked there during the day and attended law school at night but, with a family coming on, he couldn't cope with both jobs and dropped out of law school. Rick is one of the genuinely funny people of this world, great at meeting and talking to people. I knew he was wasting his time pumping gas, so I approached him about going to work for us as our ticket manager. Even though he didn't know a thing about tickets, I was sure he would learn quickly and become a great asset. We shook hands on the deal after five minutes of discussion, in which I also agreed to cut him in for a piece of Oregon Sports Attractions, which was the name under which my understanding with the hockey club gave me the right to promote other events. At the time, we were still promoting the Globetrotters and an annual professional football game, both of which were profitable.

Laycoe moved to Portland following the playoffs and was soon joined by Berlyn Hodges, who remains with me to this day. Hodges was a former professional baseball player who had acted as trainer in Victoria and came to Portland in the same capacity. It was agreed that in the off-season he would handle the sale of our program advertising. We started a season ticket campaign and were open for business.

Laycoe went to the NHL meetings in Montreal, where he arranged for the club to hold its first training camp at a place called Estevan, Saskatchewan. Then we started to try to put together a team. We had agreed to assign one of our junior sponsorships to the Boston Bruins. I will go into the details of sponsorships later; suffice it to say, for now, that for the sponsorship they agreed to loan us three players—Jack Bionda, Gordon Haworth and Larry Leach. Bionda and Haworth had played the previous season in Victoria and Leach had played in Boston, but was going to be sent down to the minors. Of the ten players we had purchased from New Westminster, only five reported to Portland. They were Art Jones, Arlo Goodwin, Gordon Fashoway, Arnie Schmautz and Ron Matthews. The other five were either retiring or weren't considered good enough. So, we had five players we owned, three on loan, none of them a goalkeeper. Obtaining one was our most immediate task.

We began hearing great reports about an amateur goalkeeper named Don Head, who had resisted all overtures to turn professional. I decided to send Laycoe to Windsor, Ontario, to talk to Head, after correspondence proved futile.

Laycoe came home to report that Head was a bit interested but wouldn't sign a contract. So I called Head with the proposal that in the event he was drafted by a National Hockey League team we would pay him a bonus equal to half the draft price of $20,000. This persuaded him to come and, at last, we had a goalkeeper.

Begging, borrowing and inviting some amateurs, we finally had a nucleus with which to open camp in Estevan, but we still needed to line up more players.

There was more than enough to do, so I remained in Portland with the understanding that I would join the team in Estevan after the camp got started. The first news out of there was that Larry Leach had broken his collarbone. Next, Bionda came down with jaundice, which might keep him out for the season. Then, Matthews was hurt. Finally, Head, on whom we had staked our team and to whom we had given a two-year contract, was looking terrible. I decided to go to Estevan.

Hodges had ordered some blankets and asked me to bring four of them to camp. I had a large suitcase, a portable typewriter and a big package of blankets. I had also been advised to bring my golf clubs since the proximity of the course was one of the virtues of selecting Estevan as a training site. Hockey players enjoy playing golf between twice-daily practice sessions. With all this luggage, I flew to Winnipeg and proceeded by bus with the Winnipeg hockey team to Brandon, Manitoba, where we were scheduled to play an exhibition game. I looked like a real hick with all that stuff draped over my shoulder and under my arms.

Then I got to Estevan and couldn't believe it. We had selected a hotel, but they couldn't even handle our team, so the players were spread around three hotels in the town. I was assigned the deluxe luxury room, as it was the only one in the place that had a shower. For a closet, there was a clothesline stretched across the ceiling. This was my introduction to Estevan. The next morning I went down to breakfast, where Bionda greeted me with, ''The rink's not bad, but the food is terrible.'' And, indeed, it was.

We turned to finding additional players. In working out our sponsorship deal with Lynn Patrick of the Bruins, we learned that he planned to turn three youngsters pro that year, one of whom was a big, young defenseman named Dale Rolfe. Boston had a firm agreement with Winnipeg and they also owned and operated the Kingston Club of the Eastern Professional Hockey League, who had first call on Bruin players. We got what was left. Rolfe was assigned to Winnipeg so Laycoe and I met with Jack Perrin, their owner, and asked him if they were planning to keep Rolfe. "No, I don't think he can make our club," said Perrin.

"If you want, you can look at him at the game in Brandon tonight," he suggested. So Rolfe, who was dressing in the Winnipeg room, took off his Winnipeg uniform, came to our room and put on a Buckaroo uniform. He played so well both Laycoe and I were convinced that we'd never see Rolfe again.

The next night, prior to a game in Estevan, Perrin asked, "Well, what do you want to do about Rolfe? Do you want to take him or should I send him to Clinton where he can play another year as an amateur?"

Laycoe started to hem and haw and get cute, so I said "We'll take him."

That's how Rolfe became a Buckaroo and one of the finest young defensemen in the league, a far better player than most on the Winnipeg roster. Bionda recovered from his jaundice and together with Matthews made one outstanding defensive combination. Rolfe, a rookie, was another, but we were desperately short of a fourth defenseman.

Our next move was a deal with Seattle to purchase Bill Davidson, a good solid veteran whom they decided to let go because they were going to turn an amateur named Gordon Tansley pro. Davidson was so incensed that Seattle would let him go that he refused to report to Portland. I tried to telephone him but he wouldn't answer my calls. Bill packed up his car, his wife and son and drove all the way from Seattle to Souris, Manitoba. On the entire trip, a distance of 2000 miles, he did not speak one word! We laugh about it now, but it was serious business at the time. Finally, Laycoe was able to persuade Davidson to join us, so we had finally put together a solid group of defensemen.

Davidson is one of those guys who couldn't shoot, couldn't skate, couldn't hit—all he could do was win. He is one of my all-time favorite athletes. I recall a tough, grueling playoff game in San Francisco a couple of years later. I sat next to Bill on the way back. "You know, Glick," he said, sucking his teeth as he spoke, as was his habit, "I don't know why we don't win 'em all. It feels so damn good when you do." That, to this day, remains the best definition of winning I have ever heard.

At center, Art Jones, who was to become the dominating player in the Western Hockey League, had a tremendous season and won the scoring championship. Gordy Haworth was adequate and when Larry Leach returned to the lineup around Christmas after recovering from his collarbone injury, we were very solid up the middle.

In Gordon Fashoway we had one of the best goal scorers in the history of hockey playing left wing. Behind him we had Arlo Goodwin. Later in the season we acquired Barney Krake and Tom Thurlby on loan from Boston.

Our most popular player—and one, undoubtedly, most responsible for our instant acceptance by the fans—was little Arnie Schmautz at right wing. At 138 pounds, he's probably the smallest pro ever to play the game. He wouldn't back down from anyone, would fight anyone, would drive them crazy checking and killing penalties. He became the sports hero of Portland.

Al Leader has told me that Edmonton had let Bill McCulley go. We signed him to play right wing and he scored 20 goals. Our other right winger was an amateur named Eddie Dudych, whom we turned pro that season.

At last we had a team.

In training camp and through the exhibition season our biggest concern was Head's performance in goal. He was terrible in practice and awful in games. In the Brandon exhibition game he actually stopped a puck with the seat of his pants. In the dressing room after the game Laycoe said, "He can't possibly be that bad, can he?" Not only did we have a heavy financial commitment to Head, but there weren't any other goalkeepers available.

Because the Coliseum would not be completed until mid-November, we had to start the season with ten games on the road, opening with six games on a murderous Canadian Prairie trip. Head was brutal the first couple of games. Then each night Laycoe would call me and each night he was a little more encouraging about Head. Finally, the team won a game and tied a game in the Prairies, then came West and won three out of four. Head looked better each game. We actually finished that road trip with four wins, five defeats and one tie, a tremendous road performance.

An amusing incident happened during that Prairie trip. You have to get this into perspective. At the time there had not been a hockey game in Portland for ten years. The club opened training camp a zillion miles from home and no Portland writers were there. The only publicity was brief daily newspaper accounts, mostly done by phone interview with Laycoe. We did not have a radio contract and our games were not carried on the air in Portland until later in the season.

Rick and I were desperately anxious for news of the team, so when the club was playing in Calgary, we decided to drive around to see if we could pick up the game on a Canadian radio station. We drove through the Southwest hills, stopping at Council Crest, one of the highest points in Portland. We were able to catch bits and pieces of the game, although with a great deal of static. It was a cold, rainy, miserable night, but we parked the car and sat there listening to the game.

Council Crest is a very exclusive neighborhood in Portland. Soon a cop drove by and spotted us in the car. He stopped, came over to our car and said, "What the hell are you guys doing?"

"We're listening to a hockey game," we answered.

"That's the most unlikely story I've heard since I became a policeman."

We tried to explain to him that we were involved with the new hockey club and we really *were* trying to listen to a game on a Canadian station. Finally we invited him into the car. You should have seen the look on the cop's face when he found out we were really listening to a hockey game!

Our home opener against Spokane drew a disappointing crowd of 5,584. The Coliseum crew was so unfamiliar with hockey that they didn't even know they had to paint the ice white. But little by little, things started to fall into place and we attracted larger crowds. New Year's night we had our first sellout, 9,843, the largest crowd in WHL history. The team caught fire and performed tremendously. It even looked like we were going to make a run at leading the league, but we finished the season with the second-best record.

We became known as the Fairy Tale Bucks. It had been predicted by a Calgary sports writer before the 1960-61 season that the Portland Buckaroos just might be the worst team ever to take the ice in the history of the Western Hockey League.

When Portland won and won and won and won, people still didn't believe it.

The hostess of a tiny restaurant around the corner from the York Hotel in Calgary made the point succinctly during the middle of the season.

Introduced to Hal Laycoe, she sort of gushed, "Oh, you're with those fairy tale Buckaroos."

A sports writer from Portland was with Laycoe at the time and he liked the tag.

It stuck. And when the championship stories were written, they referred to the "Fairy Tale Buckaroos."

Next came the playoffs. I started out as an anti-playoff man, but have come around full circle and am now a strong advocate of playoff competition in professional sports.

We won our first series from Spokane, then went on to beat Vancouver three games to one and wound up in the finals against the Seattle Totems. We won that series, the final game on the road with Head administering a 4-0 shutout. Instead of returning by bus, our usual method of transportation, we flew to Portland after the game. We were met at the airport by a mob of some 3,000 fans, who turned out with an amazing display of admiration and affection. The Fairy Tale Buckaroos won the Lester Patrick Cup their first start out of the post! I thought that demonstration was something I would never see again in my lifetime, but I couldn't know what would happen when the Portland Trail Blazers would win the championship of the NBA.

MONOPOLY—BUT WITH REAL MONEY

CHAPTER IV

THIS is a good place to examine the structure of professional hockey at the time the Portland Buckaroos entered the Western Hockey League in 1960.

There were four organized professional hockey leagues. There were six teams in the National Hockey League, the so-called major league of hockey, consisting of Toronto, Montreal, Chicago, Detroit, New York and Boston.

Next in line came the American and Western Hockey Leagues. The American League consisted of eight cities along the Eastern seaboard. The Western Hockey League stretched from Winnipeg in Manitoba through the Canadian Prairies to Calgary and Edmonton in Alberta, over to the Pacific Coast with Vancouver and Victoria in British Columbia, plus Seattle, Spokane and Portland in the Pacific Northwest. The league was organized into two Divisions with Vancouver, Victoria, Portland and Seattle comprising the Western Division.

The fourth professional league was the Eastern Professional Hockey League consisting of Sudbury, Montreal, Hull-Ottawa, Kingston, Trois Rivieres and Sault Ste. Marie.

There were also several "senior amateur leagues." They were amateur in name only as all the players were paid and under contract, just as players were in the professional leagues. Canadians are less hypocritical about the distinction between amateur and professional than we are in the United States.

In a blistering book, *Farewell to Sports,* Paul Gallico wrote: "An amateur golfer is a guy who dubs around between 80 and 110, an amateur tennis player is someone who plays on weekends and hopes he doesn't get too many shots to the backhand, which is always weak, and an amateur runner is somebody who runs for his bus in the morning and catches it. Outside of that, there are no genuine amateurs in the United States of America.'' That definition is as valid today as it was when Gallico wrote it in 1937!

Our Canadian friends simply define an amateur as a guy who's not good enough to play pro. It has nothing to do with money; the distinction is simply one of ability. Therefore a hockey player can become a professional, then revert to amateur status, and it doesn't cause a federal investigation.

The National Hockey League had a cozy little arrangement whereby it wrote all the rules, not surprisingly to its own advantage. For reasons I have never been able to figure out, the NHL was known as the ''octopus.'' What it really was in those days was a monopoly which controlled every facet of the game.

Under the rules of hockey, each professional club was entitled to a reserve list. In the NHL, this reserve list consisted of 30 players, three goalkeepers and three names on a negotiation list. In the other leagues the list was restricted to 25 players, two goalkeepers and two on the negotiation list. The list also included a voluntarily retired list for those players who had retired from the game; just in case a player ever changed his mind, the team wanted to make sure it retained his playing rights.

We had what were known as ''A,'' ''B'' and ''C'' forms. A and B were simply pieces of paper a player signed in which he agreed that he would attend the training camp of a professional club to try out for the team. A ''C'' form was a commitment from a player that when a professional club wanted to turn him pro, he would sign a contract at a stipulated figure which included his salary and sometimes a nominal bonus.

The NHL also invented another gimmick called ''sponsorships,'' which entitled each pro team the sponsorship ''rights'' to two amateur teams. This simply meant that a professional team could sponsor an amateur team and have first call on the services of every player on that team who qualified to play professionally. Thus for a nominal cost, an NHL team sponsoring an amateur team could have a farm system which would funnel players to its club with the exclusive right to turn them pro.

Let's take a look at the ramifications of that agreement. For example, in Regina, Saskatchewan, a club sponsored by Montreal, the system worked like this. Montreal would sponsor the junior club in Regina. The junior club, in turn, was entitled to sponsor two juvenile clubs. The two juvenile clubs were, in turn, entitled to sponsor two bantam clubs. The two bantam clubs were entitled to sponsor two pee-wee clubs. That meant Montreal could effectively tie up every hockey player in the city of Regina, literally from the time the kid was six years old and able to lace on a pair of skates!

It's an absolute miracle we all didn't get thrown in jail for it. When the player graduated from the junior ranks he could only negotiate to turn pro with Montreal. If the Portland Buckaroos wanted to offer him a million dollars, he still could not turn pro with any club other than the Canadiens.

Let me make it clear that the teams in the minors, such as Portland, were entitled in theory to the same sponsorship arrangement as the teams in the majors. But it didn't work that way in practice. The NHL owned or controlled practically every player. The major clubs would acquire the sponsorship rights of the minor league clubs in return for loaning them professional players to use on their own rosters. Further, the minor league teams were always on the verge of bankruptcy and couldn't afford the cost of sponsoring a junior team. Therefore, they had to negotiate those rights away to NHL clubs.

The arrangements varied from team to team. Sometimes in exchange for a sponsorship, the NHL club would loan the minor league team virtually an entire roster of players. In other cases it would only be one or two. The Buckaroos were never able to acquire more than three players on loan from an NHL team in return for sponsorship rights.

And if a minor league team ever did try to assert a little independence by actually investing money in a sponsorship, the team would get nothing but static from the NHL parent club.

In our first year we had a working agreement with the Boston Bruins, but they wanted only one of our sponsorships, there being no place left on the continent worth placing another. We made a deal to sponsor not a *junior* club but a *juvenile* club in Swift Current, Saskatchewan, hoping somewhere down the line to acquire the rights to a likely prospect. Even so, Lynn Patrick, General Manager of the Bruins, gave me a bad time for having the audacity to think we could retain and sponsor one of our own teams. And we were the only team in the minors to do so.

One of the things I was determined to do was to own as many players as possible. The history of the Portland Beavers of the Pacific Coast baseball league taught me that the loaning or optioning of players to the minors was nothing but a disaster. If the parent club sent you a good team, you had a contender. If they sent you a lousy team, you finished in the cellar. You had nothing to say about it either way. And if they did send you a couple of good ball players who started demonstrating some ability, the major league club would call them up in mid-season. That happened to the Beavers one year when Luis Tiant and Sam McDowell were both having excellent seasons and the Beavers were doing pretty well at the turnstiles. In mid-season, the Indians called both of them up. The season turned into a disaster, leaving nothing but a bad taste with Portland fans.

In short, I simply didn't want to be at the mercy of a parent NHL club, so I tried to assert our independence within feasible limits.

Managers of the minor league clubs would get together at the annual meetings in Montreal and complain mildly about this lopsided arrangement, but no one had the guts to do anything about it. We'd complain, and the NHL would laugh at us.

The following year, 1961, one of our sponsorships had gone begging. We offered it around the NHL for any consideration, but nobody seemed interested. Finally, I got a call from Punch Imlach of the Toronto Maple Leafs. He said there was a sponsorship available in a place called Unionville, Ontario, and if we would share the expense with the Maple Leafs, we could retain the minor-league rights to any player from that team, while Toronto would retain the NHL rights. I agreed. We eventually acquired two fine young goalkeepers, Dave Kelly and Rick Charron, for a price of $500 for each of two seasons. Neither of them were able to play in the NHL but they both had fine careers in the Western Hockey League. That was a bargain.

What I didn't know was that placing a sponsorship in Unionville was going to cause us a lot of trouble. There was an outstanding prospect in Unionville named Wayne Carleton. The NHL clubs had made a gentlemen's agreement that none of them would sponsor a team there just to obtain the rights to Carleton. Stafford Smythe, the owner of the Maple Leafs, gave his word to Frank Selke of Montreal that Toronto would not sponsor Unionville. So Toronto had used us as an excuse for breaking Smythe's word by placing the sponsorship in the name of Portland. We didn't learn about this subterfuge until the following summer, when all hell broke loose.

Even with this incredible monopoly on virtually every amateur player in Canada, the NHL still wasn't taking any chance that a player could escape its clutches. They had what was known as a Joint Affiliation Agreement with the American and Western Hockey Leagues. The Eastern Professional league didn't count because the NHL owned the teams in that league outright. Under the JAA, the NHL clubs were entitled to draft any player on the roster of a Western or American league club for a price of $20,000. In other words, if we somehow developed a player who had the chance to become a superstar, we couldn't negotiate much of a deal because the NHL already had the right to draft him for peanuts.

To compound the problem, there was a feud between Portland and Montreal. This involved the well-publicized brawl in a game in 1955 between Boston and Montreal, between Hal Laycoe of the Bruins, now our coach, and Maurice "Rocket" Richard. Hockey buffs know all about it. Past President Clarence Campbell of the NHL suspended Richard, preventing him from participating in the Stanley Cup playoffs. A riot ensued in Montreal.

At the end of our second season Montreal elected to draft Art Jones. The vice-president of the Canadiens, Kenny Reardon, was frank to tell the press that it was done simply to spite Laycoe. They had no intention of playing Jones in Montreal and Reardon announced, "That was one to get even for the 'Rocket'." That the brawl had taken place before anyone ever heard of Portland didn't concern him.

Well, Imlach was nothing if not loyal. As soon as Montreal announced the selection of Jones, he called time out and had a hasty consultation with Laycoe and me. "Who do you want us to draft for you?" he asked. We named Gerry Goyer, whom we had wanted in the first place and who was now playing for the Los Angeles Blades. Goyer had been their leading scorer that season. I was sitting next to Jack Geyer, the General Manager of the Blades.

"Jack," I said, "I'm sorry, but we've got to put a stop to this whole damn mess. We're going to have Toronto pick Goyer and you should have Chicago select Gene Mekylok off the Spokane roster." (He had led the league in scoring and was owned by Montreal.) "Then we can all get together and trade back for our original players to stop this nonsense."

So Toronto selected Goyer for us, but another problem developed. When we purchased the club from Mr. Hume, Laycoe sent me a letter listing the names of the ten players whose contracts we would inherit. There was an asterisk (isn't it funny how a simple asterisk has become so important in sports in recent years?) after the name of Art Jones. I asked him what that meant. He said, "The Toronto Maple Leafs own Jones' NHL rights, but don't worry because he probably won't be able to play in the NHL." This also meant, however, that Toronto owned his draft rights, and would get the $20,000 for Jones instead of Portland.

We got back to Portland and raised all kinds of hell. Our

attorney got in touch with Clarence Campbell, NHL President, and he agreed that it was a farce. Finally, there was enough pressure put on Selke of Montreal so that he agreed Jones would be returned to Portland. The only problem was that Toronto wasn't going to give back $20,000. Finally we settled for $16,000 cash. That's what it cost us for a player I had originally bought with the franchise.

All summer long we offered to sell Goyer back to Los Angeles for the $20,000 we had invested in him. I was flabbergasted when Jim Piggot decided to run with the money he obtained for the draft rights. He thought he could get as good a player on loan. What ultimately happened was that we owned two outstanding centers for a price of $36,000.

Let's go back to our first year when Head finished an outstanding season, doing a particularly great job in the playoffs. The Boston Bruins were perennial tail-enders in those years and hadn't made the Stanley Cup playoffs in more than a decade. Their whole organization came out to scout Head. Milt Schmidt, who had recently been fired as coach and elevated to assistant General Manager, practically lived with us during the playoffs. His successor, Phil Watson, scouted Head. Lynn Patrick, their General Manager, was with us through the entire final round. If they didn't know who Don Head was after all that, then no one did.

It didn't surprise me to learn that the Bruins, who had the first selection, were going to draft Head in the NHL interleague draft in June. We sure as hell didn't want to lose him for a paltry $20,000. I don't scoff at twenty grand, but it can't skate and it can't play goal. I called Lynn Patrick and said, "Look Lynn, I understand you have a lot of interest in Don Head." He admitted that the Bruins definitely intended to draft him.

I said, "Lynn, wouldn't it be worth something to Boston to have an extra choice in the forthcoming draft?"

"It sure would," he said, "but I don't understand what you mean."

"I mean," I replied, "if we made a deal to trade Head to Boston, you won't have to draft him and that will give you an extra draft for another player."

"I see what you mean," he said, "but what do you want for Head?"

"Well, for openers, when we signed him we made a deal that he'd get half of his draft price. Even though this would be a trade, I don't want to renege on my word and I want $10,000 in cash, which we will transfer to Head. Now, if you were going to draft him, it would cost you another $10,000. I want players instead, but I want a value of more than $10,000 because we're enabling you to obtain an extra first draft choice."

We worked out a deal where he would give us $10,000 in cash, plus the outright ownership of Jack Bionda, Gordon Haworth and the loan of a goalkeeper, Bruce Gamble, for the coming season. We also asked for Larry Leach, but he told us Leach had already been committed to Providence. It turned out that Leach went as part of the deal for Lynn to be able to obtain Phil Watson as his coach, who was under contract to Providence. Then they turned around and fired Watson a short time later!

The following fall, when it was time to negotiate our deal for the loan of players in return for our sponsorship, Lynn insisted that Gamble was part of the sponsorship deal. I said the loan of Gamble was part of the deal for Head. We argued about it but, naturally, Lynn won and loaned us Gamble.

An important consideration in those negotiations was that I had stipulated that if Head couldn't play for Boston, we could buy him back for $10,000. Gamble did as good a job in goal as any player we ever had for half a season, while Head turned out to be a bust for Boston. In mid-season they recalled Gamble and sold us Head. Another good deal.

From then on, Lynn spread the word throughout hockey circles that I drove too hard a bargain. While the deal turned out to be one of the best we ever made, I insist it was also a heck of a deal for Boston. They scouted him as thoroughly as any player was ever scouted and if Head was found wanting in the NHL, it was their fault and not mine. But many hockey clubs steered clear of dealing with Portland because the word was out that we had outsmarted Boston on the Head deal.

There were some other screwy things that happened in those years. There was a player on the Winnipeg list named Ray Brunel, a fair journeyman center. In our efforts to own our players outright, we made a deal with Winnipeg to purchase his contract for $5,000 and I sent Jack Perrin a check for that amount. It turned out that Winnipeg didn't own the player—Montreal did, and the Canadiens were not interested in selling him to Portland. So Brunel reverted to the Montreal list while I waited for our money. It never came. I had Al Leader intercede with the threat of taking it out of Winnipeg's forfeit bond posted with the league. About six months later I got the money back.

Recall that I said when we purchased the club that Mr. Hume insisted it be in Canadian funds and Canadian dollars were about 5% more than American dollars. By the time we made the Brunel deal the situation had reversed itself and the American money was worth about 5% more than Canadian money. I got a Canadian check back from Perrin which was worth only $4,500 in American money. So it wound up costing me $500 for Brunel and we never even owned the guy!

There were more crazy developments in those years. At the first meeting of the Western Hockey League I attended, an item on the agenda was a discussion of continuing the assistance pool. The assistance pool was a scheme nobly intended for the haves to help the have nots. It had been in operation in the WHL before we joined the league. Bud Poile, representing Edmonton, which was owned by Detroit, made an impassioned plea in which he said that the owner of the Red Wings, Bruce Norris, was a very wealthy man and did not need the help of the Western Hockey League. He said Edmonton did not want to participate in a pool, either on the receiving or on the giving end, even though it appeared they would be on the receiving end. The pool was voted out.

Coley Hall of Vancouver had contributed to the pool. He said, "I want you to know I still think it's a good idea and, although it costs Vancouver money, we are going to vote for it. But if you vote it out now, we will never vote to return it and will not contribute a dime to it again."

The next year Portland joined the league and we had fantastic attendance success. So wouldn't you know, they tried to vote the assistance pool back. Although we couldn't vote at the initial meeting, I told them that Portland favored it and urged them to continue it, but if it was voted down, we would not vote for it in the future. The first guy to vote for the pool was Poile, who had previously told us how Bruce Norris of the Red Wings didn't need our money!

Assistance pools were inaugurated at various times, all of which cost Portland some money. In general, I believe in them just as I believe in a division of gate receipts between the home team and the visiting club. But they are impractical in a hockey league with big differences in the size of buildings and wide discrepancies in ownership and the purpose of the operation.

When we joined the WHL in 1960, there was a general understanding, discussed at every meeting, that Portland was only the forerunner of other cities on the Pacific Coast to join the league when buildings became available. In fact, they passed a resolution—and it's part of the league minutes—that the WHL planned to expand to Los Angeles and San Francisco and eventually obtain major league status.

The following year a new sports arena opened in Los Angeles, and we had applications from Los Angeles and San Francisco, the SF club to play at the Cow Palace. The applicant in Los Angeles was my friend of football days, Dan Reeves. Since the Los Angeles territory had been earmarked for Jim Piggott, Reeves and Piggott made a deal to operate the club jointly. They were really after an NHL franchise in Los Angeles, which they thought they could acquire by going through the back door with the acquisition of a team in the Western Hockey League. Since Los Angeles and San Francisco were important cities in the minds of sports fans in Portland

and Seattle, their entry into the league was an important consideration to us. The small Canadian cities could see the handwriting on the wall and knew that if we took in Los Angeles and San Francisco, their own hockey days were numbered. There ensued an epic backroom battle. Since we were promised that Los Angeles and San Francisco would join the league, we expected them to keep their word, but it took a series of five meetings in Vancouver, Seattle and Calgary and some long, bitter fights, before Los Angeles and San Francisco were admitted to the Western Hockey League. As a reward for leading the struggle for them, they deserted us the first time the opportunity arose.

It had long been Al Leader's dream to bring the Western Hockey League into the NHL as a separate division. In the days when the league was struggling for survival, he had enough vision to realize that the major cities on the Pacific Coast would soon acquire new buildings capable of supporting an NHL franchise, and this kept his dream alive.

The first of the new buildings was erected in Portland, followed immediately by a new sports arena in Los Angeles. While the Cow Palace in San Francisco was old and shabby, it could be remodeled and had a good capacity. We also knew a new building was being planned in Seattle to be built following the World's Fair in 1963. A new, privately financed building was soon to be available in San Diego and the Pacific National Exhibition had plans on the drawing board in Vancouver.

You have to remember that by the early 60's the Western Hockey League had the best buildings available for hockey. At the time, there was an old and dilapidated Madison Square Garden; an old but adequate Chicago Stadium; and Boston Gardens, which was then a disgrace and still is. Fans in the upper decks have to worry about rats, among other things. Montreal and Toronto kept their old buildings in great shape, but the fact remains that the Western Hockey League had the best buildings and were ready for major league hockey.

In the winter of 1964 Leader called a secret meeting of representatives from Seattle, Portland, San Francisco and Los Angeles at the Fairmont Hotel in San Francisco. The San Francisco team was then partly owned by Mel Swig, whose family owned the Fairmont. Leader carefully outlined the situation and told us we had two choices. One was to continue as a minor league and accept the dictation of the National Hockey League. The other was to stand on our own feet and either force the NHL to accept us as a division or to form an independent major league of our own. Remember, the important consideration was that we had the buildings.

We agreed that we should follow Leader's advice and present the NHL with an ultimatum to either accept us as a division or else see us form a rival league. Leader further proposed that each club put $250,000 into a kitty to give the new league a total of one million with which to sign some of the NHL players if they refused to accept our division.

When you consider that the highest paid player in the NHL was probably earning about $25,000 a year at the time, a "war-fund" of one million would have been more than adequate to sign some of the best talent in hockey. It is still my opinion that had we signed Bobby Hull and a handful of others—and I am convinced that we could have—we would have forced a merger with the National Hockey League in nothing flat. Everyone agreed to the plan.

I returned to Portland, met with our bankers and had no trouble getting a commitment for the $250,000 Portland would be obliged to contribute to the fund. It turned out that Portland was the only team which took the trouble to do so.

If the meeting in San Francisco was secret from the press—and to my knowledge this is the first public acknowledgement that it was ever held—it was not a secret to the National Hockey League. Pressured from all sides to expand, they took immediate steps because they could see the handwriting on the wall. The National Hockey League soon afterwards announced plans for expansion.

Another interesting development soon came to light. At the

time we accepted Los Angeles and San Francisco into the Western Hockey League, Clarence Campbell, the President of the National Hockey League, wrote a letter to the Los Angeles Sports Arena Commission outlining the steps they should take to avoid indemnity if they were admitted to the NHL. In other words, while the National Hockey League was telling us they would not expand and had a contract with us in the form of a Joint Affiliation Agreement to honor the other's territorial rights, the President of the league was advising Los Angeles how to ignore it! When word of the letter was discovered, a veritable bombshell exploded.

No sooner did the NHL announce expansion plans than Los Angeles, San Francisco and Vancouver applied for admission. Portland had helped keep Vancouver alive by paying into an assistance pool. To show their appreciation they conspired to relegate us to the minors while they stepped up to the majors.

Portland was just as interested as the other teams in acquiring major league status. But we wanted our entire league to enter the NHL as a new division. We introduced a resolution to that effect at a league meeting in San Francisco, insisting that we apply as a unit. It was voted down.

Moe Tonkon, our attorney, was appointed to represent the Western Hockey League through a series of punishing and brutal meetings all over the country. After one particularly grueling meeting in Seattle, Moe and I drove back to Portland. Moe started throwing up and spitting blood. Fortunately, when I pulled off the freeway at the next exit we were near Centralia, Washington. I drove him to the hospital there and it was determined he had suffered a bleeding ulcer. He almost died that night but, fortunately, he recovered.

The clubs which intended to apply for admission to the National Hockey League were Los Angeles, San Francisco and Vancouver. They acknowledged that under our Constitution and By-laws they could not do so without our permission, as the WHL owned the territories. They agreed they would have to pay us some money but what they offered was a pittance. The National Hockey League took the position that it was a club matter and their league didn't owe us a dime. We were miles apart on the issue of indemnities.

Getting absolutely nowhere in correspondence and telephone calls with Campbell, Tonkon finally persuaded the league to authorize an anti-trust suit against the National Hockey League. That brought them into serious negotiations.

As for the clubs in our league, they also attempted to evade and postpone the issue. It was ironical that, when Vancouver applied, they didn't want any money paid to the WHL. When their application to the NHL was rejected, there they were with their greedy little hands demanding the highest indemnity we could obtain and wanting to be cut in for a full share. The other irony was that Piggott and Reeves of Los Angeles were not accepted into the National Hockey League; Jack Kent Cooke got the franchise in Los Angeles. When we finally reached a settlement with the new owners in San Francisco and Los Angeles, it was the former owners in Los Angeles who demanded—and later received—most of the money.

At the final meeting, when we were carving up the loot, Dan Reeves again demonstrated his class. The issue was how much of the money was to go to the former owners of the Blades and how much to the remaining teams of the WHL. Piggott was absolutely adamant in recovering all of the money he had lost in operating the club in Los Angeles. We were getting nowhere, when Reeves stepped in and offered to give Piggott a greater share of the indemnity so that we could reach a settlement.

We finally settled for $450,000 from each of the teams leaving the WHL, payable over a period of six years. It was my feeling then, confirmed by developments, that we settled too cheap, because the Los Angeles and San Francisco territories were absolutely vital to the National Hockey League. Without them the NHL would not be able to obtain a national television contract, the most important reason for expansion.

We were sitting in the driver's seat and we blew it.

And the people most opposed to our attempt to join as a separate division, Dan Reeves and Jim Piggott of Los Angeles and Mel Swig of San Francisco, didn't wind up in the National Hockey League.

It is interesting to note that when the NHL expanded, they added six teams—Pittsburgh, Philadelphia, Minnesota, St. Louis, San Francisco and Los Angeles.

There never was a formal application from St. Louis, but Norris and Wirtz owned a "white elephant" of a building there and you can be sure there was not going to be expansion unless St. Louis was included, so that they could get rid of their building. And that's exactly what happened.

There were several applications for the Los Angeles franchise, considered the best plum in the expansion tree. The winner was Jack Kent Cooke, because he promised to build a new arena in Los Angeles. Give Cooke credit—he put his money where his mouth was. He built the Forum to house the Kings of the NHL and the Lakers of the NBA.

Other applicants were chosen for a variety of strange reasons. The franchise in San Francisco was awarded to Barry Von Gerbig, whose qualifications were: (a) he was married to the daughter of Douglas Fairbanks, Jr., (b) he had attended an Ivy League school and dabbled in hockey and (c) he seemed like a nice kid. Those qualifications led him to screw up a franchise which has given the NHL trouble ever since.

It did bring about one of the amusing incidents in hockey. The new applicant had to play a year in our league before joining the NHL. At the end of a period in an Oakland-Seattle game, a brawl started. Fights in hockey usually start with two guys who get into it seriously, then the two benches clear and everybody else grabs a man while the first two fight it out. Van Gerbig was sitting in a seat above the tunnel entrance and immediately ran down to join the fray, to the consternation of his lovely bride, who came chasing after him. Chuck Holmes of Seattle grabbed her and informed all of his teammates, "Okay, I've got my man."

In 1965 we ended our working agreement with Boston. At the end of that season Hal Laycoe traveled to Estevan to watch the playoff games for the Memorial Cup, the junior championship of hockey. He also wanted to urge the Bruins to take a good look at Pat Stapleton, a defenseman they had loaned us for the preceding two seasons. Stapleton was a fine hockey player but the "knock" on him was that he was too short to play in the NHL. He had made All-Star in the WHL, was exceptionally good with the puck and very effective on the power play. Laycoe thought he had earned a shot with Boston.

They assured Laycoe they would take him to the Boston training camp and give him a good look. They also assured Hal they would loan us, once again, Andy Hebenton, who had had a great season with us. Hebenton was and is the all-time "iron man" in hockey with a record of 1,118 consecutive games, only interrupted several years later when he had to attend his father's funeral in Winnipeg.

When Laycoe arrived in Montreal in June, one of the many rumors floating around was that Boston and Toronto were discussing a trade involving Hebenton. Millions of rumors float around at all sports meetings and most of them turn out to be exactly that—rumors. We soon found, to our chagrin, that this one was true. Toronto was trying to unload a veteran player named Ron Stewart and they were to get in exchange Pat Stapleton, Andy Hebenton and Orland Kurtenbach. It was a bad deal because Boston would get the worst of it trading any one of them even up. Every time we looked around either Punch Imlach or King Clancy was huddled with someone from Boston, applying the pressure. The owner of the Bruins, Weston Adams, was getting involved in trades and other negotiations and he was going to make this one. It turned out that Lynn Patrick, with whom we always had good relations, advised against the deal but said, "If you're going to make it, at least save Andy for Hal and take some cash from Toronto instead." But Adams wouldn't listen and concluded the deal.

No one in hockey circles could believe it, least of all myself. And would you believe, the next day Toronto left both of them unprotected in the intra-league draft—Stapleton went to Chicago and Kurtenbach to New York. Toronto was anxious to acquire Hebenton for the farm club they were operating in

Victoria, since it was Andy's home and he had played there prior to his great career in the National Hockey League.

I immediately announced that Portland was terminating its working agreement with the Boston Bruins. To inquiries from the media, some at 3 a.m., I answered candidly, "It was because they broke their word, having promised us the return of Andy Hebenton and then reneged."

In 1964, Sammy Pollock of the Montreal organization, despite his hatred of flying, made a trip to all the minor league cities. The ostensible purpose was to scout, but it was really to prepare for taking over from Selke as General Manager of the Canadiens. He visited our office in Portland and Laycoe introduced us. It was a short but pleasant conversation. After he became General Manager I ran into him in Montreal. He stopped and said, "Harry, I know in the past there has been bad blood between our organizations." He made specific reference to the Art Jones deal.

"I just want you to know," he said, "that as far as I'm concerned it's all over and I hope that in the future we will have a good relationship. If there is anything I can ever do, please give me a call."

When we discontinued our working agreement with Boston, I recalled my conversation with Sammy and met with him. I explained that we didn't need too much help in the loaning of players, but would be interested in a deal similar to the one we had with Toronto in working out the joint sponsorship of an amateur team. Sammy immediately put one together and also sold us a player, Len Ronson.

By 1965 we had amended the Joint Affiliation Agreement with the National Hockey League to introduce a new feature called the Reverse Draft. This was ostensibly to help minor league clubs by making a restricted number of players available to them at a purchase price of $15,000, one half of the new price for the NHL draft on the American and Western Hockey League teams.

Just prior to the draft meeting, Sammy told me he wanted to purchase Tom McCarthy, who had played for us two seasons after we brought him from Boston. We wanted to dispose of McCarthy anyhow and accepted Sammy's offer of $7,500. In the negotiation we discussed some other deals, none of which materialized, but he impressed me once again with the statement, "I really want McCarthy."

I said, "Sammy, you have my word that we'll send him to you for $7,500."

The first Reverse Draft was conducted in a very small room since no one in the NHL really attached any importance to it. But there must have been a hundred guys crowded around a very small table. I found myself sitting next to Punch Imlach, who was representing Victoria, since Toronto owned the team. He also wanted to purchase McCarthy and offered me $10,000 for him. "He's already been promised to Montreal," I said. "I'm sorry you didn't ask me sooner." When it came Portland's time to announce its draft selection Punch nudged me and said, "I'll give you $10,000 for McCarthy and you can go ahead and pick a player out of the Reverse Draft."

"Sorry, Punch, I've already promised him to Montreal, but I'll tell you what I'll do, I'll give you $10,000 for Hebenton and you can go ahead and get another player." He had to think about that for quite awhile but finally he turned it down.

One of the players available for draft was Harry Sinden. He was owned by Boston on the Oklahoma City list. He was to retire from hockey and the Bruins had him pegged to coach their Oklahoma City farm club. I turned to Milt Schmidt of Boston and said, "What I really ought to do is draft Sinden just to get him away from the Boston organization."

"He can't play hockey anymore because of an injury," said Milt.

"I know that, Milt, but I should do it just for spite because I know how badly you want him to coach in Oklahoma City."

Milt said, "Harry, I wouldn't blame you one darn bit because we treated you rotten on the Stewart deal, but you would only be hindering Sinden's career because he wants to go into coaching."

"Okay, Milt," I said, "just because you asked me I won't do it, but I want you to know that if it weren't for you and Lynn I would definitely draft the guy." Sinden, of course, later coached the Bruins to Stanley Cup victories and was the coach of the NHL team in the famous first series against the Russians. I wonder what would have happened had my emotions got the best of me and we had selected him in the Reverse Draft.

While we were losing practically all of the battles in the conference rooms, fortunately we were winning most of them on the ice. There, the Buckaroos were establishing one of the greatest records in the history of professional sports.

SUCCESS ON ICE

CHAPTER V

IN the thirteen years we operated the Portland Buckaroos, we won more games than any team in professional hockey. We won the Western Hockey League regular-season championship nine times and the Lester Patrick Cup, the playoff championship, three times. My only regret, as we shall see, is that it ended on a dismal note. The final season almost spoiled the preceding twelve.

In the fall of 1961, when Los Angeles and San Francisco joined Portland, Seattle, Vancouver, Spokane and the Canadian cities of Edmonton and Calgary, the Western Hockey League for the first time in history drew more than one million fans.

Portland led the way with an all-time Western League attendance record of 294,684, plus another 38,807 for four playoff games to make a grand total of 333,491.

It was little wonder. The Buckaroos whipped off to one of the fastest starts in our history, winning eight of the first nine games, losing a few and then going unbeaten in eleven straight games, to set a record.

Portland won 19 of the first 24 games played and seemed certain to wreck every record in the league when a tragicomic chain of events started. We were forced to use seven different goaltenders, the most in a single season in the history of the WHL.

It started when Bruce Gamble, a free spirit later to star in the National League, was recalled by Boston and Don Head, hero of the '61 playoffs, returned to Portland. Shaky at the start, he was just rounding into top form when he suffered an injury and was sidelined for the season.

The game in which he was injured provided one of the most dramatic moments in hockey history. This was before the days of the two-goal-tender system and defenseman Bill Davidson, who had never played goal, was called into the nets in the final period of the game against Vancouver on February 5, 1962. Only one goal was scored against him as Portland won, 2-1.

Gamble, Head, Davidson, Seth Martin, Roy Edwards, Gerry McNamara and, finally, Al Rollins, called out of retirement, all played goal for us that season.

Despite the turmoil, we won the Southern Division Championship by ten points, tied a league record by playing 22 straight games without a defeat, and cheered a 45-goal season by a new winger named Tommy McVie, who later was to coach Washington in the National League.

The playoffs proved heartbreaking. Portland played a best-of-seven series against our most bitter rival, Spokane, but because of scheduling problems, there was no way Portland could play four home games, despite the fact that we had a better record than Spokane during the regular season.

The Buckaroos won three games at home but lost all four in Spokane, the final one by a single goal, 3-2, with Gordon Fashoway, later to coach the club, scoring twice for the Bucks.

We made it clear as we prepared for the 1962-63 season that the huge crowds of 1961-62 would result in reinvestment in the product. In other words, Portland was willing to spend money to produce a champion.

We purchased Tom McCarthy and Orv Tessier, who a season earlier had combined for a staggering 107 goals in the Eastern Professional League. McCarthy could do more than score; he was one of the toughest wings ever to play the game, and Portland had lacked toughness in the 1962 playoffs.

The Buckaroos obtained center Kenny Laufman, one of the most sought-after amateurs in the game, a scoring riot in the East. Toronto owned his rights, but Imlach said he was ours if we could sign him. Hal Laycoe and I traveled to Johnstown,

Pennsylvania and brought him in with a whopping bonus. Big center Gerry Goyer joined the club from Los Angeles via the draft deal previously described. The "Toy Tiger," Mike Donaldson, arrived from the American Hockey League via purchase from Toronto. Boston sent defenseman Dallas Smith, who later was to enjoy a long and brilliant career with the Bruins.

Don Head was back in goal and proved a first All-Star. Portland was so dominant at times that in one historic period the Buckaroos actually outshot Edmonton by a startling 23 to 0 margin.

San Francisco Coach Bud Poile, one of the best with the needle in all pro sports, called Portland "probably the finest minor league hockey team ever assembled."

The Bucks were only 6-6 after 12 games, but then played 11 straight without a loss, including an unbeaten six-game swing through Spokane, Edmonton and Calgary. But Poile had a strong San Francisco club, led by tough Orland Kurtenbach, who later was to coach Vancouver in the National League, and with 12 games to play, Portland still trailed San Francisco by three points in the standings.

Portland then went unbeaten in 10 straight, Head holding opponents to 1.5 goals a game. The Bucks whipped the Seals in the clutch, 4-1 and 8-1, and in game No. 68 of the season routed Calgary, 9-2, to win our second straight Southern Division title.

The playoffs that season were perhaps the most heartbreaking in Portland history. The Bucks met San Francisco in a seven-game series. The clubs had absolutely no love for one another and it was an emotional series. After five games, Portland led, three victories to two, winning the fifth game on an overtime goal by McCarthy.

But Portland could score only one goal in the final two games against Jimmy McLeod, who later was to star in the nets for the Buckaroos, and San Francisco went on to win the Western Hockey League championship.

The Western Hockey League became a tough six-team circuit in 1963-64. Calgary, Edmonton and Spokane dropped out and the Denver Invaders were added.

And for the first time, in a sense, the Portland Buckaroos tasted reality.

There was no real inkling at the beginning. We had said goodbye via retirement to Gordon Fashoway and Bill Davidson, but the Bucks had added National League veteran Pat Hannigan, one of the toughest wings ever, and a brilliant young defenseman named Pat Stapleton, who later was to win All-Star honors in the National League.

And in the season opener in Denver, Don Head again was brilliant in the nets as Portland won, 4-1, against a team that eventually was to win the regular-season championship.

Then Head was hurt and out for the season, rookie Dave Kelly was forced to be No. 1 goaltender, there was grousing and a lack of leadership, and on Christmas night, the Portland Buckaroos, Southern Division champions the last two years, dropped into last place.

Suddenly, we made the first major mid-season changes in our history. Doug Messier arrived. Dick Van Impe arrived. Cliff Schmautz was obtained in a trade for Hannigan, who never seemed happy in Portland.

The club sparked up and the Bucks lost only one of their final 13 games to wind up in second place. It was during this stretch that the cocky young Kelly stood the Western League on its ear by posting an all-time record of three consecutive shutouts, and blanking opponents for a record 235 minutes and 22 seconds.

In the first round of the playoffs, the Buckaroos for the first time failed to stretch a series to the limit and were eliminated by San Francisco four victories to one. None of us ever will forget the final game in the Cow Palace. Portland was leading 4-0 in the second period with a chance to send the series back to Portland, and wound up losing 6-5 in overtime.

Attendance in 1963-64 dropped to 262,843 for the regular season and to just 13,918 for two playoff games.

1964-65 was to be a season of destiny, but it wasn't totally planned that way.

The Western League really hadn't changed much, the only big difference being that Denver had moved to Victoria. When the season started, Rich Van Impe was sitting at home in Canada, suspended from an American League team. Jim (Red Eye) Hay had been cut by the Seattle Totems and a fellow named Connie Madigan, who had punched his coach at Los Angeles at the end of the previous season, was mad at the world in the American League.

All three eventually joined Portland, along with all-time National League ironman Andy Hebenton, and blended into one of the toughest and best Western League teams of all time.

The addition of Madigan was especially startling. Connie had been the all-time target of jeers in Portland when he played against us with Spokane and Los Angeles, but in his first game with the Buckaroos, Madigan scored in overtime to defeat his former Los Angeles teammates; the jeers were now wild cheers.

The Buckaroos of 1964-65 drew an all-time record of 1,118 minutes in penalties, started one of the most stunning strings in sports history—15 consecutive victories over arch-rival Seattle—and won the regular-season title by 13 points over the Totems.

Hebenton and Tommy McVie won first All-Star honors at wing and Pat Stapleton, although he played much of the season at center, was named All-Star and best defenseman in the league. Don Head was a second All-Star and so was Madigan at defense, his first such selection in pro hockey.

And then came the playoffs, with Portland looking back on three straight years of first-round elimination.

In the opener in Portland, the Buckaroos were stunned, 6-3, by the Vancouver Canucks, with young Dave Kelly nervous in the nets.

The veteran Head took over and allowed only 13 goals in nine more playoff games against Vancouver and Victoria, a 1.44 goals-against average, lowest in Western League history;

and the Buckaroos breezed to the title, winning the final game in Victoria, 3-0.

The only regret we had was that the victory could not be seen by our fans in Memorial Coliseum, who had turned out 329,773 strong for regular-season and playoff action.

The 1965-66 Western Hockey League season was, in a sense, an experimental one.

For the first time in history, teams of the WHL and the American Hockey League battled one another in an interlocking schedule. Each AHL team took a swing through the West and each WHL club journeyed through the East. Nothing much was proved. For the most part, American League teams won at home and Western League teams won at home. The games failed to do much at the turnstiles.

There were few new faces, meanwhile, in the Portland lineup. Only a pair of wingers were new on the scene, Fred Hilts on loan from Detroit and Len Ronson acquired from the Montreal organization.

Nothing much changed in the Western League standings during the regular season, either. Portland finished first for the second straight season and tied the club record of 43 victories. At home, the Bucks were close to unbeatable, winning 29, losing 5 and tieing two.

Cliff Schmautz had his finest season, winning the Western League scoring championship with 104 points, highest total by a wing in the history of the circuit; he won first All-Star honors.

Connie Madigan was voted to the first All-Star team for the first time in his career, and goaltender Don Head was named to the second team.

There was a disappointment in the playoffs. The Bucks stopped Vancouver to enter the championship finals against Victoria. Trailing three games to two, Portland had a chance to win it all with a pair of victories on home ice. The Bucks came from behind to win the sixth game, 3-2.

Then, with a chance to capture the Lester Patrick Cup before the home fans for the first time, the Buckaroos stumbled to a

5-1 series-ending defeat as old pro John Henderson was tough in the nets for Victoria.

Regular-season attendance dropped slightly, but the Buckaroos still drew 274,915 fans. And 59,062 for eight playoff tests boosted the final total to an all-time high of 333,977.

The San Diego Gulls joined the Western Hockey League for the 1966-67 season and almost immediately proved to be a strong franchise.

But it was the last season in the WHL for both Los Angeles and the California Seals, who were playing in the new Oakland Coliseum.

There were some other disturbing signs.

For the third straight year, a new all-time Western Hockey League record, the Buckaroos won the regular-season championship, this time with 89 points to 85 for a tough Seattle club. Yet, for the third straight season, attendance dropped at Portland games, this time to a regular-season total of 248,872.

This happened despite some exciting new faces—center Len Lunde, one of the most spectacular skaters in the game; Alain (Boom Boom) Caron, one of hockey's all-time top goal scorers; and rugged young defenseman Tracy Pratt, who went on to a long National Hockey League career.

Connie Madigan won first All-Star honors the second straight season and Art Jones, nipped by Seattle's Guyle Fielder for the scoring title in the final game of the season, was voted to the second team.

In the playoffs, the Buckaroos couldn't buy a goal and lost four straight to Vancouver in the first round. Three of the losses were really tough, 1-2 in overtime, 2-3 in overtime and 2-3.

But it was still the first time a Portland club ever had been eliminated in four straight in the playoffs.

Two noteworthy events followed the 1966-67 season. The first was the expansion of the National Hockey League, meaning that the WHL was reduced to five cities. I knew that the loss of Los Angeles and San Francisco were going to be devastating. They were considered major league cities by our fans, who particularly enjoyed it when we beat them on the ice. But I still thought hockey had a viable future in Portland because it was such a great game and we had established a winning tradition.

The preceding February, when he received his NHL franchise, Jack Kent Cooke had asked me to meet with him to discuss the possibility of my going to work for him, and to get permission to talk to Laycoe about the coaching job. I gave him permission to talk to Laycoe as soon as the playoffs were over, which was the same position I took with Pittsburgh when that club also expressed interest in obtaining Hal as their coach.

Here I made one of my most monumental mistakes. Instead of encouraging Laycoe to go, I persuaded him to stay. Hal and I had had our personal differences, but I thought—and still do—that he was a great hockey coach. I didn't want to lose him but I didn't want to stand in the way of his coaching in the NHL, which had long been his ambition.

I told Hal that I was going to attempt to buy the club from Lane, Foreman and the Gamble estate. The club had already bought Clay Brown out for a price of $15,000 on an original investment of $1,500, not a bad profit. I told Hal if I could find the needed financing, I would cut him in for exactly the same ownership I would obtain. Hal thought it over and rejected the NHL coaching offers to remain in Portland.

Let me make it clear there were never any serious differences between us and the owners. Lane and Foreman left us alone to operate the club. And well they should. We gave them victories on the ice and profits on the bottom line.

I have previously mentioned the bank loan of $75,000 we got when we first bought the club. Would you believe we paid it off in one year? At the end of that season Lane and I marched down to the bank with a check for the balance of our loan. The officer, Carvel Linden, was flabbergasted. "This restores your faith in people," he said.

Each succeeding year we were able to declare a dividend for

our stockholders. So, all in all, owning the hockey club proved a rewarding and enjoyable experience.

Since Portland had proved to be the best franchise in minor league sports, I thought any team in the NHL would jump at the offer to buy the club. My first choice was Montreal, but Sammy Pollock was committed to a new franchise in Houston in the Central League.

Next, I approached Punch Imlach of Toronto, always one of my favorites in hockey. Punch expressed enthusiasm and told me to talk to Stafford Smythe, the President and principal owner. Smythe also indicated interest, but kept stalling around.

That year I passed up the meetings in Montreal and Laycoe went by himself. I told him to check around quietly with some other NHL teams to see if there was any interest. One day, talking to Billy Reay, the coach of the Chicago Blackhawks, he mentioned that Portland might be for sale. When Hal told Billy we were dealing with Toronto, Billy told him, ''I think you're talking to the wrong people. They're strapped for cash.''

When Laycoe relayed this information to me I was startled. Toronto was one of the most successful franchises in the sport and never had an empty seat. They had a five-year waiting list for season tickets. What I didn't know was that Smythe and Harold Ballard were stripping the club of cash. Ballard later served a jail sentence and Smythe was under criminal indictment at the time of his death.

Reay told Laycoe that Chicago might have some interest. The new Governor of the Blackhawks was Billy Wirtz, son of the Arthur Wirtz who, together with Jim Norris, had operated the International Boxing Club. (Norris had died the preceding winter following a stormy expansion meeting.) I got in touch with Wirtz by telephone and he asked me to send him our financial statements. He was also impressed with our lease at Memorial Coliseum. I didn't think it was all that great, but considering that the Chicago Stadium charges the Chicago

Bulls something like 25 percent for rent, our lease in Portland looked appealing to him.

Arthur Wirtz and his other son, Mike, came to Portland to investigate. We met in Tonkon's office and I outlined my proposal. I said we had an option to buy the club for $300,000. My proposition was that Wirtz advance us the money in return for a third ownerhsip of the team, with the incentive that he could use Portland as Chicago's number-one farm club. Chicago had previously operated in Buffalo in the American League but had ended that agreement on a note of recrimination. The Blackhawks also owned Dallas in the Central League.

Wirtz said, "If I'm going to be a partner, I want to sit with both feet under the table. I'll put up the $300,000 if I can have 50 percent interest in the club." That was all there was to it, and in a matter of an hour we closed the deal. Laycoe and I divided the other 50 percent equally.

We took Arthur and Mike to dinner that night. The following morning we signed the papers to conclude the deal. Then I asked Wirtz if he wanted to see his new office. We walked down the street, he looked around for a few minutes, said, "so long," and headed for the airport.

The agreement Tonkon drew up obligated us to repay the loan at the rate of $50,000 a year including interest. If they didn't like the way we operated the club, all they could do was fire us from our jobs. We still retained our stock. I thought it was a pretty good deal.

All of my dealings with Chicago were with Tommy Ivan, the General Manager. I would have breakfast with Billy each year at Montreal and that was the extent of it. I could never even reach him by telephone. Tommy and I got along fine and he is a good friend, although we did have a couple of problems later on involving the purchase of two players, Dennis Kerns and Rick Foley. Chicago continued to operate Dallas as their development club and, since we owned practically all of our players, we only needed the loan of one or two players a year to be competitive.

Before the 1967-68 season, the Buckaroos made perhaps the

boldest trade in our history. Laycoe had never been overly enchanted with Head and he sent the veteran goaltender to Seattle in exchange for Jimmy McLeod.

It was bold because Head had been the unquestioned hero of playoff championships in both 1961 and 1965, but he also had knee problems and wasn't getting any younger. The Buckaroos were looking to the future, and in the long run, the trade paid off for Portland.

The Western League was down to five teams in 1967-68. Los Angeles and San Francisco had gone to the National League but Phoenix joined the Western circuit, and WHL teams played the second and last interlocking schedule with the American Hockey League.

We had many new faces that year. Center Norm Johnson, one of the all-time scoring leaders in the WHL; defenseman Dennis Kearns, who later was to star in the National League; speedy winger Mel Pearson; defenseman Wayne Smith; wing Andy Hebenton, back with the Bucks after a trade with Phoenix; and a goaltender named Marv Edwards, who had been a star in Eastern amateur circles.

There were some great individual performances. Art Jones won the Western League scoring title and was voted the league's Most Valuable Player, a first for the Buckaroos. Connie Madigan was first All-Star at defense for the third straight year.

But the big story was written by goaltenders McLeod and Edwards. Edwards posted a goals-against average of 2.36 to set an·all-time Western League record. McLeod was even better, 2.23, but failed by about 100 minutes of action to qualify for an official record.

As a result, the Buckaroos won our fourth straight Western League championship with a 40-26-6 record. Yet it was the fourth straight season of dropping attendance, 228,924 for the regular season, while San Diego was setting a new league paid attendance mark of 311,857.

The playoffs were exciting, then disappointing. The Buckaroos stopped San Diego four victories to three in the first round, winning the final game 3-2 in overtime. Then Seattle whipped the Buckaroos for the title four victories to one, a pair of the losses coming in overtime. Head had temporary revenge against his old teammates by shutting out the Bucks, 4-0, in the final game.

The 1968-69 Western Hockey League season, the last with Laycoe as coach, was in many respects the most staggering in our history.

It was a six-team league, Denver rejoining the WHL, and look at these facts:

Portland finished 40-18-16 for an all-time Western League record of 96 points in the standings.

The Buckaroos scored 84 power play goals, an all-time record for professional hockey.

Portland finished with 805 scoring points (goals and assists) for an all-time high in the Western League.

Veteran center Art Jones won his third WHL scoring title with a then career record of 114 points.

Wing Bill Saunders scored 53 goals, the most ever scored by a Buckaroo in a single season.

In the nets, Jimmy McLeod posted a goals-against average of 2.29, the lowest in the history of the Western Hockey League.

Four Buckaroos, Jones, McLeod, Saunders and Connie Madigan, won first All-Star honors, Madigan for the fourth season in a row. Norm Johnson and Dennis Kearns were named to the second All-Star team, giving the Buckaroos the 1-2 centers in the WHL.

And the Buckaroos blazed to their fifth straight Western Hockey League regular-season championship, one of the finest records in the history of pro hockey.

Yet attendance was down for the fifth straight season to an all-time low of 209,224, although six playoff games added 45,296 for an overall total of 244,520.

It was enough to make me wonder. We were a living contradiction of the theory that the more you win the better you draw.

In the playoffs, the Buckaroos for the second straight year eliminated the San Diego Gulls, four victories to three, in the first round.

Then the Bucks were wiped out in four straight in the finals by the strong Vancouver Canucks, already girding for the National League. In the final two games, Canuck defenseman Marc Reaume scored in overtime in both contests to earn Vancouver 3-2 and 2-1 victories.

In the summer of 1969, Laycoe resigned to accept a coaching position with the Los Angeles Kings.

Frankly, I was glad to see him go. Although we had enjoyed success together in operating the Buckaroos, we had some notable differences, which we managed to keep quiet. Although I respected him and admired him as a coach, he just wasn't my kind of guy.

My first problem with Laycoe came at the end of our very first season, when the "Fairy Tale" Bucks won their first Lester Patrick Cup.

During the playoffs there was a league meeting in Seattle and I attended en route to a playoff game in Victoria that evening. The league held a luncheon following the meeting and among those present were Admiral Bergen and Muzz Patrick, respectively the President of Madison Square Garden and the General Manager of the New York Rangers. Everyone in the room except me knew they were going to Victoria to talk to Laycoe about coaching the Rangers.

I was naive enough to believe that if a National League team wanted to talk to our coach, they would at least show me the courtesy of asking permission. Besides, it was in violation of the tampering clause of the Joint Affiliation Agreement. I also operated under the naive belief that, if Laycoe were going to discuss another coaching offer, he would at least have the courtesy to talk to me about it first. I had told him I'd never stand in the way of his going to the NHL.

I found out, of course, and challenged Hal about what I considered a serious oversight. We straightened out that problem. Although they discussed the job with Laycoe, the Rangers never officially offered it to him. At any rate, we signed him to a new two-year contract and Hal, with his monumental ego, demanded that we include in the release a clause stating that he had turned down a job with the Rangers in order to remain in Portland. We accommodated him and that seemed to make him happy.

Two people Laycoe intensely disliked in hockey were Bud Poile and Coley Hall. When we first joined the league, Hall owned Vancouver and Poile was coaching Edmonton. When San Francisco came into the league, Hall sold his Vancouver club at a sizeable profit, even though he didn't own any players, acquired San Francisco and hired Poile to coach the Seals.

At one league meeting Hall was raving and ranting when Laycoe interrupted him.

"What the hell you even opening your mouth for?" said Hall. "You're not an owner and you don't even know what it is to meet a payroll."

That crack prompted Laycoe to want to own some stock in the club and when we bought Clay Brown's stock, we gave part of it to Hal as a bonus. He later got his kicks by being able to tell Hall he was, indeed, an owner. It is absolutely incredible that later Laycoe went to work for the two of them when Hall wound up owning the Vancouver club in the National Hockey League with Poile as the General Manager.

The thing that finally broke my pick with Laycoe involved our acquisition of the team with the Blackhawks. He became increasingly convinced that we had assumed personal commitments which, in fact, we had not. Nothing our attorney or I could tell him altered his position. Finally, after much personal recrimination, Tonkon and I bought his interest.

After that episode, I was determined to get rid of him, and when Jack Kent Cooke called the following spring for permission to discuss the Kings' coaching job with him, I not only gave my permission, I did so with the fervent hope that he would hire him. And he did.

Then came the ultimate blow. Before Hal had taken the Los Angeles position, we had had an offer from Larry Reagan, the General Manager of the Kings, for Dennis Kearns, a young defenseman whom Gordy Fashoway had discovered while playing in a Senior League in Kingston, Ontario. We had signed him and brought him to our training camp, but Laycoe didn't want to turn him pro. Fash and our trainer, Berlyn Hodges, had finally persuaded Hal to keep him. Kearns proved to be one of the best defensemen in the league, great with the puck and the power play, and later became a defenseman in the National Hockey League.

Los Angeles was seriously interested in Kearns and offered to trade us a defenseman named Leo Amadio. Hal turned the deal down because he thought it was a bad trade and because he didn't think Dennis was ready to play in the NHL. He rejected the deal at least half a dozen times before taking over as coach of the Kings.

After Hal had signed with the Kings, he returned to Portland and told me how grateful Cooke was that I had given him permission to join the L.A. club without asking a thing in return. "Cooke knows you're working with Chicago," Hal told me, "but he said to tell you if you ever need anything from Los Angeles, he'll be glad to help."

Hal insisted that he was going to continue to represent Portland at the hockey meetings in Montreal because his contract in Los Angeles didn't start until July 1. I said, "Okay, come along with Fash and me." On the plane he came over to us and announced that he was now interested in acquiring Kearns for Los Angeles.

"I thought you said he wasn't ready for the NHL when they offered us a deal before," I said.

"Well, I'd like to have him," Hal said, "and we'll offer Amadio." Fash and I looked at each other in utter amazement. "You're telling me you're offering us the same deal now that you're with Los Angeles that you rejected while you were with Portland. Forget it."

"In that case we're going to draft Kearns," said Laycoe.

"Over my dead body," I told him.

When we got to Montreal, Laycoe asked us to meet with Reagan in his suite. Fash and I went and he once again offered us the same deal. I reminded them about my conversation with Laycoe after he took the Los Angeles job. "Cooke said you guys wanted to help us. If this is your way of showing your appreciation, please don't do us any more favors."

The NHL draft rules stated that only one player could be drafted from a WHL team. Since Chicago had finished last in the standings that year, they had an early draft choice and we arranged a deal, the kind I dislike but one that was necessary in this instance, for them to draft Bill Saunders so as to prevent Los Angeles from drafting Kearns. The Blackhawks took Saunders to training camp and he almost made the club.

Fashoway, a Buckaroo original as a player and one of hockey's all-time goal-scoring leaders, had been scouting for us since his retirement. We were the only team in the minors to employ a full-time scout and Fash did a great job. He was the logical choice to become the coach as we prepared for 1969-70.

It was a seven-team league that year, Salt Lake City joining the WHL. For the first time in six seasons the Buckaroos finished in second place.

But you couldn't fault Gordy. The Bucks posted a 42-23-7 record and finished with 91 points in the standings. That point total would have been good enough for first place in five of the six previous WHL seasons, but the Vancouver Canucks had a powerhouse and wound up with 102 points, an all-time Western Hockey League record.

The playoffs of 1970 were the most memorable in Portland history—for misery. We played our final three games with only one defenseman, Connie Madigan, from the regular season.

Jerry Korab, the muscle of the team and later a National League star, and Mike Donaldson, a steady veteran, both missed every game in the playoffs, Korab with a knee injury and Donaldson with a broken ankle.

Paul Terbenche, another future National Leaguer, played three games and was out the rest of the way with injuries.

Rick Foley, the rest of the muscle on the team, and another National Leaguer-to-be, Dennis Kearns, were injured in the eighth playoff game and were out for the season.

We had to call in three defensemen on loan.

Announcing the appointment of Gordon Fashoway as head coach of the Portland Buckaroos.

Portland still beat Seattle four victories to two in the first round, but it was no surprise that Vancouver won in the finals, four victories to one.

And what a touch of irony to the ending.

Laycoe had been fired from Los Angeles midway in his first season and was named Vancouver coach just before the playoffs. He is listed officially as coach of the championship team.

In the fall of 1970, the Vancouver Canucks started play in the National Hockey League. And for the first time in history, the Western Hockey League had all United States cities—Portland, Seattle, San Diego, Phoenix, Denver and Salt Lake City.

The season was perhaps Portland's most spectacular. Yet it was the season in which the handwriting on the wall as to the future of the Buckaroos became clear.

Consider the situation:

For the eighth time in 11 years the Buckaroos finished in first place.

We won more games, 48, than any team in Western League history and set a new all-time record for points in the standings with 103.

Portland, with 306 goals, was the highest-scoring team in Western League history.

Seven Buckaroos scored 23 or more goals, and five finished in the top 10 in scoring, led by first-place Art Jones with 114 points.

Judging by penalty minutes, the Bucks were the roughest WHL team of all time—they drew a new record, 1,302 minutes off the ice. Big defenseman Rick Foley led the way with a league individual record of 306 minutes.

In 11 seasons in the WHL, Portland had won more games (458) than any other team in pro hockey—Montreal's Canadiens were second for that period with 424.

And yet attendance in 1970-71 stagnated to 220,529, an average of 6,126 a contest in a city where the average once had been close to 9,000.

The playoffs were marred by the suspension of All-Star defenseman Connie Madigan for flattening a referee in San Diego; Madigan was out the rest of the way.

Because we ultimately won the Lester Patrick Cup, I can look back upon that suspension as an amusing incident, but at the time, it was a disaster. Madigan had belted the referee in the third game of the series. Gene Kinasewich, who succeeded Leader as president of the WHL for a short period, rightfully suspended Madigan for the remainder of the playoffs.

But he also suspended Norm Johnson and Rick Foley for the next two games for their part in the incident, and that wasn't right. It was almost as if he were deliberately trying to deprive the Buckaroos of the chance to win.

For that, and other reasons, candidates from the hallowed halls of Harvard need not apply for the presidency of any league of which I am a member.

I was in New York with my basketball scout, trying to sign a couple of second-round draft choices, when Kinasewich announced the suspension. Stu Inman and I had adjoining rooms at the Hilton Hotel.

While we were talking to one player and his agent, a call came from Fash informing me of what happened. I sent them to the next room while I talked to Fash, then rejoined the negotiations.

Then a call came from Kinasewich and I sent them back to the original room. This went on for a couple of hours. We must have played musical rooms ten times while I took part in the basketball negotiations and conducted my hockey business.

Yet Portland stopped San Diego four victories to two in the first round and then swept past Phoenix four victories to one in the finals. We had our third Lester Patrick Cup, thanks in part to the sensational goaltending (2.03 goals-against average) of Jimmy McLeod. The trade of Don Head to Seattle for McLeod had paid off in full, as McLeod shut out Phoenix, 5-0, in the final playoff game.

The Portland Buckaroos are presented the Lester Patrick Cup in 1971.

But even the playoffs drew only 49,509 fans for six games, an average of 8,252 a contest in a city in which the playoff average once had been 10,000.

There was, indeed, handwriting on the wall.

As the 1971-72 season got under way, there was good news and bad news.

High-scoring winger Cliff Schmautz returned from the Philadelphia club of the National League. And there were some good acquisitions, most notably defensemen Barry Long and John Van Horlick, plus center Guyle Fielder, top scorer in Western Hockey League history.

But we lost veteran center Norm Johnson, who retired to coach Spokane's amateur team, and All-Star goaltender Jim

McLeod, who moved up to the St. Louis Blues of the National League.

The loss of McLeod, until he returned with 13 games to play, seemed to hurt most.

Portland, with 301 goals, still was the highest-scoring team in the league. And the team was a winner, 38-31-3. But we dropped to third place for the first time in the club's history, Denver finishing first and Phoenix second.

There were some individual highlights. Jones won the Western League scoring title for the fifth straight season with 124 points. It was the fourth straight year in which he had scored 114 or more.

In addition, Cliff Schmautz sparkled with a 40-goal season, and with Connie Madigan and Bill Saunders was named to the second All-Star team. (Jones was first All-Star center.)

Buckaroos players sip champagne from the Lester Patrick Cup.

But attendance dropped to an all-time low of 201,861, an average of just 5,607 a game.

The first round of the playoffs against Phoenix was one of the most memorable of all time for Portland. The Bucks were trailing one victory to two. Then we stopped Phoenix 4-3 in overtime in Portland, 3-2 in overtime in Phoenix and finally 6-2 in Portland to advance to the finals.

Jimmy McLeod, who had returned from St. Louis, was brilliant in the nets. In one overtime period in Phoenix he stopped an incredible 24 shots.

In the finals McLeod couldn't do it alone, and Denver won the playoff title four victories to one.

The five playoff games in Portland attracted just 34,613 fans, an average of 6,923 a game.

The end seemed nearer.

By the end of the 1971-72 season it didn't take a genius to see that there was trouble on the horizon. I had known that the loss of Los Angeles and San Francisco was going to be devastating. To compound the problem, Vancouver left to join the NHL and the league did not have a Canadian city. This was the final blow to the Western Hockey League and the future was very dim.

I still believe that the loss of the so-called ''major league'' cities, Los Angeles and San Francisco, plus the loss of our lone remaining Canadian city, Vancouver, were primarily responsible for our declining attendance. Another reason, ironically enough, was that we were winning too much and were starting to bore people. But I could never believe that the answer to the problem was to start losing hockey games, because any fool could have easily arranged to do that by getting rid of our good players.

With Tonkon representing the league as legal counsel, we formed a Relations Committee to negotiate a deal with the National Hockey League to keep the WHL alive. We held meetings all over the continent and finally signed a document on June 7, 1972, known as the WHL-NHL Agreement.

This agreement provided that in any future expansion of the National Hockey League at least half the new teams would have to be members of the Western Hockey League. The NHL simultaneously announced that they intended to expand to 24 teams by 1980, which meant that every team in the WHL meeting NHL qualifications would eventually achieve major league status.

The agreement also provided for indemnity amounts to be paid to surviving teams in the Western Hockey League as teams moved to the NHL. It also provided that the NHL would help the league survive by operating development clubs in the WHL.

It further provided—and this was crucial—that if a Western League operator didn't want to take a chance on losing money, a National Hockey League team must operate the club without any loss to the WHL operator.

Following the NHL meetings in Montreal in June of 1972, Moe Tonkon and I arranged to stop in Chicago for a meeting with Arthur and Billy Wirtz. I wanted to make them aware of our problems in the forthcoming season. For the first time we were going to need more help on the ice than they had been providing and, secondly, our financial situation was precarious.

We had met all of our annual payments to the Blackhawks but still had to make one more to repay the $300,000 loan completely. We made the final payment by discounting our note from Vancouver for the indemnity they owed us and assigning it to the Blackhawks. So we were completely clean. But it definitely looked like we were going to lose money the following season.

Had I known then what I know now, I would have sold the club immediately. We still owned players' contracts which were worth some money. I could have left with a profit and clean skirts. But I was determined to see us through another year, at which time I could turn the club over to a new operator, who need not fear losing money because he would be protected by the WHL-NHL Agreement. The prospect of operating a development club, with little voice in the type of team we put on the ice, didn't appeal to me.

In Chicago Arthur, Billy, Moe and I met, then Arthur excused himself and we went to lunch with Billy. He seemed sympathetic to the problem and was sure that he could provide the help to see us through the season. We left with the understanding that we would discuss it further but that help would be forthcoming.

All summer I tried to reach Billy on the telephone but he simply does not return calls. I made Tommy Ivan aware of the problem and the fact that our season ticket sale was very poor. Finally, at a meeting of the Western Hockey League in Seattle on September 7, I was assured that I would be hearing from Wirtz. I waited two days without a phone call. Finally, at the end of the meeting I asked the Governors for a private session. I said that I regretted very much having to tell them what I was about to say but that the situation in Portland was desperate. I said I didn't want to pull out at this late date as the season was almost ready to start, but cautioned them that I might have to do so.

The response was overwhelming. Bobby Breitbard stood up to say that Portland had been a valuable member of the league and, if necessary, he would personally provide the funds in order for us to operate the following season. All the other members were sympathetic to our problem and said that they would do everything to help us out.

This was not unusual because the league had loaned money to both Seattle and Denver in the past to permit them to complete the season. Indeed, the Portland Hockey Club had co-signed notes for the funds the league lent them.

Again, it would probably have been wise to sell the club and get out right then and there. I could have sold enough players' contracts to refund the season ticket money and walked away with a nominal profit. But my pride and stubbornness got the best of me and I decided to see the club through the season.

I determined I was not going to run a campaign, warning, "If you don't come out to support us, you're gong to lose your hockey club." The Portland Beavers had done that for years, which had turned me off and had never helped their situation, anyhow.

To compound the problem we started off with a terrible year on the ice. Hoping to spark attendance by creating new interest among the fans, we played an interlocking schedule with the Central Hockey League. The Central League, with Dallas, Tulsa, Fort Worth and Omaha, had mostly youngsters who played wide open, free-skating aggressive hockey. But the names meant nothing in Portland and attendance dropped to an all-time low.

There was another reason for the falling attendance. For the only time in history a Portland hockey team finished in last place with 21 victories, 39 defeats and 12 ties. And for the first time in Buckaroo history, I had to fire a coach. The team was off to a 5-13-1 start so I had to replace Fash. There was practically a rebellion among the players. Three of the leaders called me to a meeting to say there was no way they could continue. It was especially tough because Fash was not only, in my opinion, a good coach but he was a close personal friend. But he had let the club get away from him. Fash was a throwback to the old-time method of coaching which was "give the guys hell." It simply wouldn't work with modern hockey players. Fash took it like the man he is and said he would do anything he could to help us through the season as Director of Player Personnel. I replaced him with Berlyn Hodges, who had formerly been our trainer and was now the vice-president of the club, who also worked in my basketball operation. He had very little coaching experience; he gave it his best shot but nothing worked.

Even before the season started, All-Star goalie Jimmy McLeod had jumped to the World Hockey Association. Connie Madigan was in the throes of his periodic bickering and in January we sold him to St. Louis, partly to pay off a debt we owed Philadelphia, for Cliff Schmautz.

There were a few individual highlights. Art Jones finished third in scoring with 89 points. Cliff Schmautz scored 30 goals and so did Andy Hebenton—at the age of 43. But for the first time ever, there were no playoffs.

By November our situation was desperate. We already owed the league $15,000 for an unpaid playoff assessment from the preceding season. I couldn't meet my payroll of November 30 and had to borrow another $8,000 from the league in order to do so.

On December 8 the league held a special meeting in Scottsdale, Arizona. The minutes of the meeting show: "Mr. Glickman indicated that his relationship with the Chicago Blackhawks had deteriorated and he was unable to consummate an agreement whereby the Blackhawks would provide the necessary funds to meet the anticipated obligations of the Portland Hockey Club. Mr. Ivan, who was in attendance representing the Chicago ownership, and Mr. Glickman were excused from the meeting to see if an agreement could be reached. Jim Cullen, also representing the Chicago Blackhawks in this matter, also met with Mr. Ivan and Mr. Glickman and returned to the meeting indicating that the matter of financing the Portland hockey club through the 1972-73 season had been resolved."

Cullen was a trouble shooter for the National Hockey League in his role as attorney for the St. Louis Blues. There were reports that he was seeking Clarence Campbell's job as President of the NHL, as Campbell was due to retire. We got on the telephone with Arthur Wirtz and reached an understanding that they would take over all obligations in return for complete control of the franchise. They were also supposed to pay Tonkon and me $50,000 for our stock in the club. When we finished talking to Wirtz, I turned to Tommy and Cullen and said, "Now have we got this thing understood thoroughly?" Everyone agreed. We shook hands on the deal and went back into the meeting to report that there were no further problems.

Our understanding with Wirtz was that he would send Jim Cullen to Portland to complete the documents with Tonkon and then would deliver the money. I went to Pittsburgh to investigate the possibility of a new tennis league, which was to be the forerunner of the present World Team Tennis.

In Pittsburgh I received a call from Tonkon informing me that Wirtz had reneged on the deal. I had already issued the December payroll, which represented the Christmas checks for the players, so I told Moe the best thing I could do was jump out of the twentieth story of the hotel. I don't believe I've ever known a lower day in my life.

The next morning I jumped on a plane for Seattle to see Bill McFarland about my predicament. Bill had succeeded Leader as President of the WHL. Bill, on his own and without the permission of the league, gave me a check to underwrite the payroll. I signed a note for it. He was a first-class guy all the way around. The players' Christmas checks weren't going to be bouncing all over town.

The league met again in New York on January 30, 1973. The minutes record: "The President reviewed the financial situation of the Portland Hockey Club and indicated that the agreement between Arthur Wirtz and Harry Glickman, which had been negotiated by James Cullen (representing Arthur Wirtz) and Harry Glickman at our meeting in Scottsdale on the 8th of December, 1972, had not been consummated due to a subsequent disagreement between the parties. On January 13, 1973, Arthur Wirtz transferred certificates numbers 6 and 7 of the Portland Hockey Club's stock, representing 250 shares and one half of the stock issued, to the WHL. The letter of transmittal indicated the transfer of stock was a 'donation' to the WHL. The matter of the Board of Governors of the WHL accepting this donation was discussed and a motion was made by San Diego to accept the donation. After an examination of the buy and sell agreement between the two groups of stockholders and the Portland Hockey Club, and further discussion, it was resolved that this matter be tabled until the WHL Special Meeting in San Diego February 5.''

I went to the meeting in San Diego at the mercy of my partners in the WHL. Remember, Portland had come to the aid of other clubs when they had been in distress. I proposed to the league that they give us $300,000 cash, which would enable us to complete the season and pay all of our bills. At the end of the season I would turn over to the league the franchise and the contracts of all of our players, which still had some value. Also, I would turn over the indemnity agreement which provided that the teams remaining in the WHL could receive up to $800,000 from the WHL-NHL Agreement.

This was exactly the deal I had previously proposed to Arthur Wirtz and his response was, "It isn't worth the paper it's written on." Here was a document that had been negotiated over a period of two years in meetings all over the continent. One of the parties to the negotiations was his own son, Billy, and one of the signatories to the document was Clarence Campbell, President of the National Hockey League, and here was Wirtz telling us it was all in vain because "the document wasn't worth the paper it was written on."

Prior to the San Diego meeting, a loan had been arranged with Seattle First National Bank in the amount of $230,000 to meet past due and future obligations of the Portland club and to insure its continuation through the 1972-73 season. In order to secure the loan, a letter of credit was obtained from the Southern California First National Bank guaranteed by Robert Breitbard of the San Diego Hockey Club. An agreement was entered into by and between the WHL member clubs and Breitbard indemnifying him as guarantor of the letter of credit. The Western Hockey League now owned our franchise. I was simply to operate it until our fiscal year ended May 31. McFarland and a committee came in, reviewed our books and authorized all of our expenditures.

I went into a shell and didn't even try to promote. It was a burden even to go to the Coliseum to watch the team play.

By May I was out of hockey, with mixed feelings. I loved the sport and admired the players. I think they were some of the greatest athletes with whom I have ever been involved. But that feeling was soured when, at the end of the season, some of the players said that the owner had "deserted the ship" in the middle of the season. I viewed those remarks as unfair, because

I could have let their Christmas checks bounce, dissolved the club and walked away leaving them unemployed. I'm sure they wouldn't have said what they did had they known all the facts.

It was also the only time I have ever felt I was treated unfairly by the media; one of the interviews with the players had taken place by tape recorder in a tavern. That situation was salvaged, however, by Doug LaMear of KGW-TV, who did a half-hour special which I think permitted me to answer all the critics.

So, we were out of hockey, but I will always be proud of the record we wrote. There was still plenty to do in another sport.

THE MAJORS—BUT IT DIDN'T COME EASY

CHAPTER VI

AS already noted, I was rebuffed in the 50's in my first attempt to obtain a franchise in the National Basketball Association. Once into hockey and enjoying some success, I lost most of my interest in the NBA. The games were not shown on national television, and only occasionally, when the hockey team was playing in San Francisco or Los Angeles, would I take in a basketball game.

Each year, prior to or after the annual hockey league meetings in Montreal, I stopped in New York to visit with my old friend Pete Rozelle. Among my other unfulfilled ambitions, I wanted to bring a National Football League team to Portland. In 1964 we had a ballot measure for the construction of a domed stadium, which was narrowly defeated. I thought then—and still do—that an NFL franchise would be a tremendous success in Portland. Of course, I think an NFL franchise would be a tremendous success in just about any metropolitan area in the country. Pete kept telling me that the league would expand following the merger with the American Football league, but insisted that the city they wanted in the Northwest was Seattle and encouraged me to check it out. "We definitely want to go there and we want to see you involved," he told me. I did check it out briefly, but Seattle has never been my favorite town and I couldn't get too excited about the possibility.

I didn't get serious about the NBA again until 1969. When Jack Kent Cooke was talking to me about going to work for him, our first meeting was held prior to a basketball game between the Lakers and the Boston Celtics. It was a great game, I thoroughly enjoyed it and my interest in the NBA was renewed. By 1969 the NBA had expanded to include Phoenix, Seattle and San Diego, all good rivals for Portland, in addition to San Francisco and Los Angeles. Under Walter Kennedy's stewardship, the league expanded from nine to 14 teams and was to increase even further.

The first thing I did was to get in touch with Kennedy by telephone. He said that the league had further expansion plans, and he thought there would be serious interest in Portland; he encouraged me to proceed.

I filed our preliminary application and started pounding the pavement looking for investors. Walter had indicated that the purchase price of a new expansion franchise would be somewhere in the neighborhood of two and one-half million dollars, more than the price paid by the last teams to enter the league. I had previously obtained a list from Mark Hatfield, when he was Governor of Oregon, of people who might have the financial resources to invest in a professional sports franchise. I used this list, together with one given me by Gerry Pratt, financial editor of The Oregonian. But Pratt warned me, "Remember, people in Oregon with a lot of money want anonymity, not notoriety." How right he was!

My first plan was to try to organize a group of ten local investors to form a sub-chapter S corporation. Each of them would put up $100,000 for 10% of the stock for a total of one million dollars. The remainder of the purchase price was to be borrowed from a bank, with the money guaranteed by the personal signatures of the investors. Down the line we contemplated a public stock offering to repay the bank loan, with the initial ten investors to retain enough of the stock to have operating control of the team.

After a lot of work I was able to put a group together. Each of them had the financial capability to borrow a million dollars at the bank on his personal signature alone. I made inquiries at the bank about the possibility of obtaining the needed loan and was assured it would be no problem with the group we had.

A league meeting was scheduled in Philadelphia at the time of the All-Star game on January 20, 1970. There were franchise applications from four cities—Portland, Buffalo, Cleveland and Houston. The scuttlebutt was that the league would accept two of four at the meeting in Philadelphia.

Going back, for a moment, to our public stock offering, I am certainly no genius in the realms of high finance. I was aware that it would be necessary to file a registration for a stock offering with the Securities and Exchange Commission. I was advised that it could take up to six months before final approval, and it would be necessary to obtain interim financing until the SEC registration was approved. One of our potential investors was Dave Sherman, who worked in an investment house in Portland. He dug up a guy who was willing to provide the interim financing and all he was asking in return was an option to buy some of the stock.

From the investor's point of view it wasn't a bad deal, because in the event of a problem with our SEC permit he felt he could always sell the franchise to one of the cities that was not accepted and easily get his money back.

In the meantime, I started my own campaign. I called every owner in the league whom I knew personally, had introductions to others and wrote all of the rest. At the time, a fellow named Harold Pollin had just moved to Portland and I met him on a social occasion. He was the brother of Abe Pollin, owner of the then Baltimore Bullets and a member of the Expansion Committee. I sought his help in obtaining Baltimore's vote and his answer was, ''I'd sure love to see Portland in pro basketball and if I can't deliver my brother, who can I deliver?''

One of my most outspoken supporters was Franklin Mieuli, owner of the Golden State Warriors. I first met Franklin when he was involved in the ownership of the San Francisco 49ers and produced their television and radio braodcasts when they played in Portland. Franklin had attended the University of

Oregon for only one year, but he was still a loyal Duck booster, and that didn't hurt my cause, either.

Just prior to the meeting in Philadelphia, Cooke called and invited me to a meeting in Los Angeles. He said he was Chairman of the Expansion Committee and wanted me to come down to have lunch. The only other representative there was Bobby Breitbard, who had recently acquired the NBA franchise in San Diego. Bob owned the Western Hockey League team in San Diego and had constructed a new sports arena there. Bob and I became good friends and I knew he would be in my corner. In fact, it was partly through his encouragement and optimistic outlook for the NBA that I eagerly sought the franchise.

When I arrived at the Forum, Cooke informed us that the other member of the Committee was Dick Bloch of Phoenix, who couldn't be there; but Cooke had his proxy. Jack started off by saying that this was not going to be "bargain basement" day in the NBA and any thought of buying a franchise at a price of two and a half million dollars was ridiculous. Jack felt that the price should be five million dollars, and I thought he was ridiculous. Nothing much came of the meeting except that I left very discouraged by the kind of numbers they were talking about. I called Kennedy to tell him about my meeting with Cooke. Walter told me that the Expansion Committee of the entire league had met and that the purchase price was going to be three million dollars. He advised me to come to Philadelphia with our prospectus and financial projections. He seemed generally optimistic about our chances.

I proceeded to Philadelphia with my attorney, Moe Tonkon. We arrived and encountered tough break number one. Walter Kennedy had laryngitis! I mean, the poor guy was sick and couldn't talk above a whisper. I attended one of his press conferences where his method of communication was to whisper in the ear of Carl Scheer, his executive assistant, who would relay the answers to the waiting reporters. I knew Walter was on my side, but at this meeting he was going to be of absolutely no help.

We cooled our heels Sunday and Monday while the usual rumors floated around. The applicant for the franchise in Houston was Alan Rothenberg, who was Cooke's attorney for the Lakers. We discovered that Alan and I were fraternity brothers and so developed a good relationship. Thus, I had a pipeline into Cooke's thinking, which was not encouraging. The applicant for Cleveland was Nick Miletti, who owned the Cleveland franchise in the American Hockey League. I had met Nick on my visits to Montreal and considered him a friend. I had never heard of the guys from Buffalo.

Finally, we were told the Expansion Committee would meet Tuesday afternoon and would invite all four applicants to appear individually and then collectively. When Tonkon and I appeared for our interview with the Expansion Committee, we were told that the purchase price would be four million dollars and the expansion teams would not share in television revenue for a period of three years. We were not given any of the details of how the new clubs would be stocked with players.

I absolutely blew my top. I told them I thought they had dealt with us in bad faith. I told them that the Commissioner had assured me as recently as the day before that the purchase price was going to be three million dollars and that the new teams would share in television revenues. I explained that I had been a good partner in the other league in which I had operated and wanted to be a good partner in the NBA, but only on the basis of full equality, sitting with both feet under the table with every other club in the league. I made it clear that Portland had no interest in joining the NBA or any other league in which we wouldn't receive a full share of the television revenue. I still hold that position and think the ABA teams should have received a full share of television revenue when they joined our league.

I was followed by Tonkon, who said, "In all my 45 years of practicing law, I have never been dealt with so shabbily. Here you have a Committee which has invited our application, the Commissioner has told us what the purchase price would be and now you intend to go back on your word. Under the circumstances, Portland would have no interest in joining.''

The other three proposed applicants apparently all said the same thing, for when we were invited to appear as a group, all of the teams gave the same answer—they were not interested at that price or under those conditions.

We had been given tickets to attend the All-Star game that evening. I returned to my room, called the airlines and found we could jump on a plane to Portland if we could get to the airport in about twenty minutes. Moe and I threw our stuff into a suitcase and hailed a cab. It was snowing something terrible and we barely made it to the airport. As we raced out of the hotel, I ran into a newspaperman from Seattle, who later wrote, ''Harry Glickman left Philadelphia with smoke pouring out his ears.'' I was glad to get out of Philly, but the time was to come when I'd be glad to return.

I came home convinced that my dreams of putting Portland into the major leagues of professional sports were completely shattered. During the next several days I received calls from ABA teams asking us if we would be interested in joining their league. But I felt it was tough enough getting involved in a player war in the dominant league, so I had no interest in the ABA.

Then I started getting telephone calls from the members of the Expansion Committee. I recall talking to Sam Schulman, the owner of Seattle, for about an hour in a very heated conversation. I was adamant about one thing, we weren't going to join the league unless we could come in as full partners. I cooled off enough to have an intelligent conversation with Abe Pollin, who had replaced Cook as Chairman of the Expansion Committee. I said, ''Abe, if they want to bump the price a little bit because they think they're going to get a lucrative television contract, maybe that makes a little sense, but if it happens, we definitely want to share in that contract.''

Abe and I eventually worked out the deal by which the

Expansion teams were finally admitted. The purchase price was to be 3.7 million dollars; the new teams would receive a full share of television revenue and would be equal partners in all other respects. Furthermore, if there was to be a merger with the ABA, as was rumored at the time, our purchase price would be reduced to the same amount paid by the ABA teams when they joined the NBA.

My enthusiasm renewed, I got in tough with my investors. Frankly, the new purchase price scared hell out of them. This was the winter of 69-70 and the stock market had gone down the tube. Interest rates were soaring and money was extremely tight. On a visit to the bank where I had previously been assured we would be able to borrow a million dollars without any problem, I was told that the money simply wasn't available. The only money we could obtain was Eurodollars, which, if we wanted to borrow a million dollars, would be discounted by 3% and carry a 12% annual interest charge. No matter how I put a pencil to my projections—and they were very conservative—there was no way our team could break even with that kind of interest expense.

It was back to the drawing board and time was running short. This was late January and the next meeting of the Expansion Committee and of the league was scheduled in Los Angeles on February 6. In a last-ditch effort, we put a meeting together including representatives of almost every investment house in Portland. This group was spearheaded by a gentleman named Sheldon Jones. I explained my predicament, and said I thought Portland could get a franchise and be successful in professional basketball. Was there any way they could come up with the dough? I am pleased and proud to say that within 48 hours we had commitments for the entire purchase price of 3.7 million dollars. Our only problem was that we didn't have any interim financing. The guy Sherman had produced backed away because the plan now was to accept all four teams which had applied. This meant that if we did not get SEC approval for our securities registration, he would be out the interim financing of $750,000. I was frantic, but I couldn't blame anyone for not committing to that kind of money with such a high degree of risk.

The deal I had worked out with Pollin called for a down payment of $750,000 and a further payment of $750,000 within 90 days. The balance of the purchase price of 2.2 million was to be paid in four annual installments of $550,000. Where would I get it?

He kept asking how my plans were proceeding and I kept telling him everything looked good. He said there was a gentleman interested in the Portland franchise and if I had any financial difficulties to get in touch with him. I asked who it was and he said I knew the fellow casually but he would not disclose his name.

While all this had been going on I had been in touch with Dick Vertlieb in Seattle. Dick and Don Richman had organized the Seattle franchise and interested Sam Schulman in becoming one of the investors. Richman left Seattle after one season and Vertlieb became the General Manager. He later got into a beef with Shulman and was either fired or resigned—there are two versions of the story. At this time he was selling securities in Seattle.

Now I called Dick and explained my problem—no interim financing. I asked him if his Seattle investor would have any interest in putting up the interim financing. He called back to say he would not be interested on that basis. Then Tonkon called Dick and the upshot of the conversation was that we invited them to come to Portland to discuss a possible deal. They were to fly down that afternoon, Wednesday, February 4. Remember, the league meeting to award franchises was only two days away. I went to the airport not knowing whom to expect with Vertlieb. Well, it was Herman Sarkowsky, who happens to be my wife's ex-brother-in-law! I couldn't believe it. I had met Herman once or twice but didn't know anything about him except that he was supposed to have done well in the home building business in Seattle and Portland. I drove them to Tonkon's office for the meeting. We discussed the matter at some length and then invited Dick and Herman to have dinner with us.

We had an important hockey game scheduled at the Coliseum that night and I always thought the team couldn't play if I wasn't there. I was anxious to get the dinner over with as fast as possible. The result of the meeting was that Sarkowsky flatly rejected any part of a public stock offering, and wouldn't get involved on the basis of interim financing. He did say, however, "If you're having trouble putting this deal together, I'll be glad to take over the whole thing provided I can get two other friends of mine to go in with me." The proposed deal was that he would take 75% of the club and sell 25% of that to each of his two friends. Of the remaining 25%, George Rickles and I were to receive 10% as a finder's fee, and the other 15% was to be offered to the original Portland investors if they still wanted to come in. If not, Sarkowsky would commit to the other 15% and would sell it to five friends. This arrangement enabled us to form a sub-chapter S corporation.

I drove Herman and Dick back to the airport. They left with the understanding that Herman would call me the following morning after talking to his two "friends." "They" turned out to be Larry Weinberg of Los Angeles and Bob Schmertz of New Jersey, both personal friends of Herman who had also done very well in the home construction business. Herman called the next morning to tell me that Larry had given him an immediate "yes." Weinberg was a great fan of the Lakers and loved basketball. He said Schmertz was somewhere on the East Coast in his private plane but that they had left messages for him at every airport where he might conceivably land. I told Herm I had to jump on a plane for Los Angeles that afternoon but to let me know as soon as he heard from Schmertz. He said he would get in touch with Tonkon's office and that Moe would call me at my hotel as soon as I arrived in Los Angeles.

I flew to Los Angeles and checked into the Beverly Hillcrest Hotel on Pico Boulevard. The meeting of the Expansion Committee that evening was at the Beverly Wilshire Hotel, a few blocks away. There were no messages waiting for me and I couldn't reach Tonkon at his home. So I didn't know where I stood. I went over the the Beverly Wilshire for the meeting, which was held in Abe Pollin's suite. Among those attending were Fred Zollner of Detroit, Pollin, Tommy Cousens of Atlanta and Carl Scheer, representing Kennedy. I had based my projections on what I knew of current NBA salaries and my experience with hockey expenses. I thought it was a realistic but conservative budget. They all congratulated me on the soundness of the plan. Zollner questioned the numbers I had put down for player salaries but Scheer reminded him that I had taken the average salaries in the NBA that season and had increased them by 10% per year. Little did I know they would increase by more than 100% in less than a year! I explained that we had a firm commitment for a public stock offering but that we had no interim financing.

Needless to say, this didn't please them because there would be no money up front. Tommy Cousens of Atlanta entered the conversation. I had never met the gentleman, but he had heard of me and heard of Portland and wanted us both in the league. "I will personally put up $250,000 for you," he said, "but you've got to have the people in Portland put up something. Can't you see if they will come up with an equal amount so there will be at least a down-payment to the league for the franchise?" It's superfluous to add I fell in love with Cousens in exactly five seconds. I told them I would call my people in Portland and get back to them that evening. I went into Pollin's bedroom to use the telephone and called Sheldon Jones to report what had happened. He couldn't give me any encouragement that any cash could be forthcoming immediately from the group in Portland. I left Pollin's room to seek out Nick Miletti to find out what his plans were. As I pressed the elevator button I remembered that I had left my raincoat in Pollin's bedroom. When I went back to retrieve it, there was a telephone call waiting for me from Sarkowsky.

"Did Moe get in touch with you?" he asked.

"No, I haven't heard from Moe or anyone else."

"Well, I finally heard from Bob Schmertz. We reached him at an airport in Bermuda and he is anxious to go along. As soon as I heard from him I called Moe and took off to go skiing."

"Great," I said, "you called just in the nick of time because I just left the committee meeting thinking we were dead."

I went back to the room and said, "Hey guys, time out, there's a whole new deal."

I explained that we were now going to have a privately financed company. Their ears perked up when I told them the people were financially responsible and that the money would be paid as scheduled. I was instructed by Abe Pollin to report to a meeting of the entire league at noon the following day, to be held in the offices of Sam Schulman at the National General Corporation on San Vincente Boulevard. I called Herman back to tell him I had to produce evidence by way of a letter of credit in the amount of $750,000 at noon the following day. He assured me I would get a call from his banker in Tacoma the following morning and everything would work out fine.

I waited until 10 o'clock the following morning and didn't hear from the bank in Tacoma, so I placed a call there. Herman's contact told me to get in touch with their sister bank in Los Angeles, the United California Bank, and a gentleman named Hugh Darling would take care of whatever I needed. I called Darling. He had never heard of me, Sarkowsky, the NBA or anything else. He called Tacoma, called me back and said, yes, he would handle my problem. Normally when you talk $750,000 to bankers you shake them up pretty well. This didn't seem to phase him. He said he would not issue a letter of credit but would give me a letter guaranteeing that the bank in Tacoma would issue the funds. He thought this would be satisfactory to the league. I asked if he could send the letter by messenger. He said they didn't have any available, so I would have to go down to the bank to pick it up. He gave me directions. The bank was located downtown; in Los Angeles, that's a million miles away from Beverly Hills.

His branch was on Spring Street and he instructed me to drive down Wilshire Boulevard, but I thought I would outsmart them by driving down Olympic, since there seemed to be less traffic. But Olympic does not run into Spring Street and I was completely lost.

Eventually, someone pointed me in the right direction and I arrived in the bank's parking lot at 11:15. I still had to report to National General by noon. I went up to Darling's office and he was in a heated long-distance telephone conversation. He waved me to a chair where I sat biting my nails for about ten minutes. When he finished, he started asking questions about Portland and the National Basketball Association. I conveyed to him the urgency of the letter, said I would be happy to invite him to a game when we played in Los Angeles, but I wanted to get the letter and get the hell out of there. He dictated it to his secretary, but when she brought it over to him to sign, he noted a typographical error and instructed her to retype it. I said, "Don't bother with that, just initial it and give me the damn letter," which he did.

I left the bank at twenty minutes to twelve and headed up Wilshire Boulevard for National General. Going through red lights, I made it to National General at 12:05 and raced up to the meeting room. I handed my letter to Abe Pollin, who told me he had been worried about my lateness so had asked for a recess while he went to the john. He remained there until I arrived with my letter. Abe then instructed me and the representatives of the other three teams to come back at 3 p.m., when we would get their decision.

Nick Miletti and I went to lunch, and when we returned were met by Ray Patterson, then General Manager of Milwaukee, who told us we were in. He said that Abe Pollin would come out to welcome us formally to the NBA and to look surprised when he did so.

Soon Abe arrived, congratulated us and told us we were in the National Basketball Association. Kennedy said there was to be a big press conference at the Forum and invited us to accompany him to it. I told him I wanted to hold my own press conference via telephone with all of the media in Portland. So I returned to my hotel, calling or responding to calls from all the newspapers, radio stations and television stations in Portland and throughout Oregon.

I checked out of the hotel about 7, just in time to race for the airport to catch a plane home. When I checked out, the telephone operator told me she had counted more than 40 telephone calls either placed or answered by me. I guess that covered all of the media, some of them several times.

The next morning we held a press conference at the Coliseum, one of the most pleasant with which I have ever been involved. My parting shot was that I hoped that in late spring—and in the same week—the Portland Buckaroos would win the Lester Patrick Cup of the Western Hockey League and Portland's yet unnamed team would win the championship of the National Basketball Association.

Both of these hopes were to materialize, but not in the same week or the same year. The Buckaroos would win the Lester Patrick Cup at home the following season, but it was to be seven years before the Portland Trail Blazers were to be crowned champions of the NBA.

PATIENCE IS A TOUGH VIRTUE

CHAPTER VII

THE next weeks were a welter of activity. As a compiler of lists—if I don't write it down I'll forget it—I had identified 300 things to be done prior to the college draft only six weeks away. But first I felt obligated to call all of the people who had been involved in our original financing plans to ask if they would be interested in joining the new group as minor stockholders. All of them declined but were ecstatic over Portland's entry into the NBA and wished us nothing but success. There was only one exception. That was Ed Steidle, the president of Meier & Frank Company. Steidle had been earmarked for 5 percent of the franchise. He was upset with the new arrangement, for reasons which I have never been able to understand. I explained that we couldn't obtain interim financing and there was no other way to go with our local group. Nevertheless, over the course of the next couple of years, he complained repeatedly about the "absentee ownership" of the new franchise.

On Monday, it was time to go to work on my list of more than 300 items. It included everything from selecting a name for the new team to choosing the colors of our uniforms, finding new office space and adding personnel to our new operation.

The most pressing and immediate problem was the upcoming college draft. We had exactly six weeks to get ready for this important event. The draft was scheduled to be held on March 23, immediately after the regular season. The NBA was at the height of its war with the American Basketball Association and the bidding for playing talent was astronomical. Since we could not be sure of obtaining the franchise, I had not been able to do anything definite about scouting the colleges that season. My most urgent problem was to find a scout.

Bob Houbregs, the General Manager in Seattle, recommended Donnis Butcher, the former coach of the Detroit Pistons. I called Bob early Monday morning and obtained Butcher's telephone number in Detroit. I was just in the process of placing a call to him when a telephone call came in on the other line from Art Johnson of the San Francisco 49ers. First, he congratulated us on the new franchise. Next, he said, "You must be looking for a scout."

"Nothing serious," I replied. "I'm only desperate."

"I might have just the guy for you," he said. "Ever heard of a fellow named Stu Inman?"

"He used to coach at San Jose, didn't he?"

"Yes," said Art, "he's a good friend and I think he would do a good job for you. He's now working for Converse in the Bay area."

I called Stu immediately. He had been following professional basketball very closely in his job with Converse and so knew the makeup of all of the teams in the NBA. He also watched a lot of college games and was familiar with the talent available in the draft.

Stu flew to Portland the next day. We discussed our philosophies of building a team in the NBA and discovered we were in complete agreement as to how to proceed. The most necessary attribute is patience, a virtue with which I am not abundantly blessed.

But I was determined going in that we would build this team slowly via the college draft in order to become a contender. I hear of these geniuses in professional sports who attain instant success with their uncanny ability to make trades. Show me one who has ever won a championship. The closest is George Allen of the Washington Redskins, whose motto is "The future is now." Allen did get the Redskins into the Super Bowl once, but he has never won it and I predict he never will.

The organizations I most admired in professional sports were the Minnesota Vikings and Dallas Cowboys in the National Football League and the Montreal Canadiens in the National Hockey League. The Vikings and Cowboys were both expansion teams who had played in Portland during their first year of operation. They were terrible but they built steadily and patiently. Once they achieved success, they were able to remain contenders over a long period of years and, in fact, still are. This was the formula I wanted to use for the Trail Blazers.

It's not that I consider trades unimportant; but there has never been a genius in our business who has traded his way to a championship. Colleges offer us the greatest farm system ever devised. We not only obtain highly skilled and talented basketball players each year, but we also obtain instant attractions at the gate.

One of the best examples of a team that was floundering and then was put together via the draft is the champion New York Knicks of 1970 and 1973. Their mainstays—Willis Reed, Walt Frazier and Bill Bradley—were draft choices. Once they had put this lineup together Eddie Donovan, their General Manager, found himself in the fortunate position of being able to make a trade for Dave DeBusschere. That cemented their lineup and enabled them to win two NBA championships.

Stu and I, in complete agreement, decided that he should fly immediately to Salt Lake to scout a game that night. He was on the road constantly over the next six weeks observing college talent. It was impossible to watch all of the players we wanted in such a short period of time, but Stu had great contacts in the college coaching ranks and so was able to obtain a pretty good line on the talent available in the forthcoming draft.

We started a contest to select the name of the new team by forming a committee to pick the winner. Something like 300 different names were suggested. The name "Trail Blazers" was not the overwhelming choice but it seemed to be everyone's second choice. Because there was no agreement, Trail Blazers became our name almost by default.

In an effort to stimulate interest in professional basketball while dickering to obtain a franchise, I had booked three league games in Portland featuring the Seattle SuperSonics. In those days it was common practice for NBA teams to play some of their home games in other cities. I had made the deal with Dick Vertlieb, then General Manager of the Sonics, who assured me he would give me one fair game, one lemon and one really good attraction. The three opponents were Detroit, Milwaukee and the New York Knicks. Detroit drew a crowd of about 4,000 for a terrible basketball game. The other two attracted capacity crowds and, in fact, were the biggest gross gates Seattle drew all that season. They also turned out to be pretty good games and sparked some interest.

The next task was the selection of a coach. I obtained recommendations from Stu, Pete Newell, who was then General Manager of San Diego, Red Auerbach of Boston and several others.

Red Auerbach was to become one of my closest friends in the NBA. I could always call upon him for advice and he was never too busy to offer it. Red has as many enemies as friends, but I think most of it is sheer jealousy. He was never the most gracious winner, and his habit of lighting a cigar when a victory was assured turned a lot of people off.

But how can you argue with the guy's record? Nine championships in 11 years of coaching the Celtics and two more as General Manager—that's a record I predict will never be surpassed. Dynasties are a thing of the past in professional sports.

I submit that coaching a team of such enormous egos as Bill Russell, Bob Cousy, Tommy Heinsohn and all the rest—and keeping them mentally hungry enough to want to win more—that's coaching. Whatever the secret, Red had it. He can also be a delightful companion in a Chinese restaurant and a helluva competitor on a tennis court, either as partner or opponent.

My first choice for the coaching position was Bob Boyd of the University of Southern California. I met with him twice and was convinced he was ready to accept the job. He had formerly been set to leave USC for the Lakers, but on the day they were to make the announcement Boyd declined, deciding to stay with the Trojans. He did so again in the case of Portland. My next choice was Tex Winter of the University of Washington, but he also declined the job.

I interviewed, among others, Maury John of Drake; Tom Nissalke, then Larry Costello's assistant in Milwaukee; Jim Loscutoff, a former Oregon player who had played with the Celtics for many years and was then coaching at a small school, Boston State; and Rolland Todd of the University of Nevada at Los Vegas.

I was intrigued by Loscutoff because he had been a great player at Oregon, but, other than Auerbach's, I couldn't get another strong recommendation for him. I first met with Todd at an early breakfast meeting in Chicago and was impressed. Upon further research I was pleased to learn his college teams played fast-break, exciting basketball, running up high scores.

We finally decided to wait with the decision on the coaching job to concentrate on the college draft.

In the meantime, a couple of league meetings were held in which we had to complete the details relating to the franchise. I went to a meeting in Chicago with $750,000 in my briefcase but had one heck of a time giving it away. Rumors of an impending merger with the ABA were rampant. The attendant controversy relative to the payment by the expansion teams, should ABA teams come in at a lesser price, forced me to withhold payment until the matter was settled. Abe Pollin finally resolved the problem in a handwritten document and I was able to distribute the money.

I returned to the problem of forming the team.

There are vintage years in sports. In the National Football League they still talk about the incredible draft of the 1951 college crop which brought into the NFL such great stars as Ollie Matson, Hugh McElhenny, Billy Wade, Ed Brown, Gino Marchetti, Les Richter and many more.

The 1970 college draft in the NBA will go down as one of the greatest in history. How would you like to have a team with

Bob Lanier and Dave Cowens at center, backed up by Sam Lacey and Clifford Ray; Rudy Tomjanovich, Garfield Heard and Curtis Perry in your front line and Geoff Petrie, Calvin Murphy, Pete Maravich and Nate Archibald in the backcourt? Those players all came in the 1970 college draft and some of them weren't even first rounders.

By the time of the draft, Houston had forfeited its franchise when Alan Rothenberg lost his backers among the Texas millionaires. Coin flips between Buffalo, Cleveland and Portland determined our choices in the college and expansion drafts. Cleveland won the right to select first in the college draft and Buffalo the right to select first in the expansion draft, so Portland received the second choice in both drafts.

We had the eighth pick in the first round of the college draft, which was conducted in a small press room at Portland's Memorial Coliseum. When we announced our selection of Geoff Petrie, there was a stunned silence among those present. No one had ever heard of the guy and the headlines reflected it by saying, "Portland drafts Geoff Who?"

We finished the draft and were congratulating ourselves on completing our first important job when I received an urgent call. It was Chuck Kaufman, one of Petrie's agents. One of the reasons we had selected Petrie was that he had signed a contract with the league to play in the NBA. I thought it of utmost importance to be able to sign our first draft choice. It developed that many players, including Lanier and Tomjanovich, had done the same thing under the same agents, Norman Blass and Kaufman.

My introduction to professional sports agents came with Kaufman's call informing me that Petrie was unhappy with the contract. He had received a much better offer from the New York Nets of the ABA and didn't intend to honor the contract he had signed with the league. Now it was my turn for stunned silence. I told Kaufman that I thought we had a valid contract, but that we would be happy to discuss the matter; I suggested that he and Petrie come to Portland as soon as possible. They came a couple of days later accompanied by the assistant coach at Princeton. We met in Moe Tonkon's office. I explained that signing a contract was the same as giving your word and we expected them to live up to their word. If they wanted to break it they would have to take it to court and our lawyers advised us we would win. I further said I was not prepared to renegotiate the contract but I would consider adding some bonus and incentive clauses. We eventually worked out a deal and the bonuses that we added earned Petrie an additional $17,000 the following year, to my mind not an inconsiderable amount of money.

Next, Stu joined us permanently as our Director of Player Personnel.

After further research and interviews, we settled on Rolland Todd as our coach, who quickly earned the nickname of "Mod Todd" because of his stylish dress. The thing that impressed me about Todd was his knowledge of the NBA. I was amazed at how little attention college coaches paid to professional basketball, its players and the league. Todd had played a season in the old ABL and was intimately familiar with the pro game and most of the players.

Next, we had to prepare for the expansion draft to be held in New York on May 11. The first position we wanted to fill was center. Our first choice of the available talent was Leroy Ellis of Baltimore. Meanwhile, Pete Newell of San Diego arranged a deal with Red Auerbach of Boston to make Larry Seigfried available in the expansion draft. Pete told us that if we would take Seigfried, he would immediately trade Jim Barnett to us. We liked Barnett not only because he could play both forward and guard but also because he was a "name" in Portland as a former star at the University of Oregon.

In order to make the Barnett deal we had to arrange for the other teams to pass on Ellis. We told Bill Fitch of Cleveland that if he would name a player we would pass on him to get Cleveland to pass on the player we named. (We sometimes play funny games in our drafts.) Fitch named someone other than Ellis, so we were able to work out the deal to get both Barnett and Ellis. We also obtained forward Ed Manning from Chicago; guards Rick Adelman from San Diego and Stan McKenzie from Phoenix; and center Dale Schlueter from San Francisco. We traded our third selection, Gerry Chambers, to Altanta for forward Gary Gregor.

In retrospect, there were to be some rocky roads for the Trail Blazers in our "Seven Years to Glory," as one of our films is titled. But our first NBA season, 1970-71, was fun.

In addition to the veterans from the expansion draft and Petrie, we also picked up Shaler Haliman in a deal with Chicago. Three other rookies were chosen to round out the ball club—Walt Gilmore of Ft. Valley State, our second-round pick; Ron Knight, a forward from Los Angeles State, a fifth-round choice; and guard Claude English from Rhode Island, our seventh-round selection.

All of this so impressed the national magazines that they commented in the season previews:

"This may be the worst group of draft choices ever taken."

"Don't worry, San Diego, Portland will break all your first-year records for futility."

"On paper, this appears to be the weakest of the expansion franchises."

Fortunately, the Trail Blazers were not impressed by the national magazines. We proceeded to win 29 games, the second-best record for an expansion team in NBA history. We finished with better records than fellow expansion clubs Buffalo and Cleveland.

Todd had promised to excite the fans. He did. Portland gave up 120 points a game, still the worst defensive record in our history; but the Blazers, running and gunning, also scored 115.5 points a game. That's still the all-time offensive high.

In one of the most exciting games ever played in Memorial Coliseum, the Blazers trailed the Atlanta Hawks 64-80 at halftime. Portland scored 82 second-half points to win 146-131.

From left, Harry Glickman, executive vice president of Portland's Trail Blazers; Gov. Tom McCall; Walter Kennedy of New York, National Basketball Association commissioner; and Herman Sarkowsky, Blazers president.

The Blazers blew out the New York Knicks before what was then the largest crowd in history, 11,868.

We had a five-game winning streak in mid-season and closed out the first NBA campaign with another five-game winning streak.

Then there was Petrie. He simply scored 2,031 points, still a club record. He was the second guard in NBA history to score more than 2,000 points in his first season, and Geoff shared NBA Rookie-of-the-Year honors with Dave Cowens of Boston.

Our attendance gave hints of things to come. Although our first league game against Cleveland drew a disappointing crowd of 4,273, in our final game of the season, against Seattle—a game which meant nothing in the standings—the Blazers were cheered to victory by a wild turnout of 11,140.

At the end of the season, we assessed our situation. Although our fans were exhilarated with our unexpected success of 29 victories, 16 of those wins came over Buffalo and Cleveland; in the NBA schedule that year we had to play each other 12 times. So we had won only 13 games against the rest of the league. We had to make some changes.

We finished with the worst record in our Conference, and had to flip with Cleveland for the right to the first selection in the 1971 college draft. Cleveland won the toss.

Everyone's choice was Sidney Wicks of UCLA, the college player of the year, and several teams were trying to make a deal with Cleveland to obtain his rights. We had some conversations with Nick Miletti and Bill Fitch, so they knew of our interest, but we had nothing to offer in the way of playing talent. The week prior to the draft Miletti and Fitch were suddenly unavailable. We were meeting in our office on the Saturday before the draft, figuring whom we would take, when Miletti called. He and Fitch were in Los Angeles trying to negotiate a deal with Jack Kent Cooke. They asked if we were still interested in Wicks and we told them to jump on the next plane to Portland.

Nick was desperately short of cash. He was playing in a decrepit old building in Cleveland but was making plans for the fantastic new arena he has since built there. I have never divulged a player's salary and rarely the cash involved in any transaction, and I don't intend to do so here. Suffice it to say, when the draft was held the following Monday Cleveland's selection of Austin Carr of Notre Dame was met with mild surprise. It should have been, because it didn't happen by accident. We selected Wicks.

The acquisition of Sidney Wicks, who had led UCLA to the last two national championships, had an immediate impact. Our season ticket sales doubled. Seattle had obtained Spencer Haywood toward the end of the preceding season, so we scheduled home-and-home rookie games in the two cities as we concluded our rookie camp. Believe it or not, the rookie game in Portland attracted a capacity crowd at Memorial Coliseum. Our future looked bright.

Wicks went on to win Rookie-of-the-Year honors in a landslide vote. He became the eighth rookie in the NBA history to score more than 2,000 points and he hauled in a team-leading 943 rebounds.

Before we drafted him, or indeed even before we knew we could obtain him, Sarkowsky and I had met with Wicks' two representatives in Los Angeles, Sam Gilbert, the godfather of UCLA basketball, and Willie Naulls, a former UCLA great who had also enjoyed success in the NBA. After we drafted Wicks, he was signed by Weinberg and Sarkowsky through a series of meetings with Gilbert and his lawyer, Ralph Shapiro.

Sidney arrived for fall camp where I scheduled him for an appearance at a dinner meeting in Vancouver, Washington. He was to meet me in my office so we could go together. No Sidney. I waited—no Sidney. I tried to telephone him—no answer. Finally, already late for the appearance, I drove to Vancouver thinking Sidney would show up on his own. He never did. I finally reached him that night and he said he had a cold. I told him he should have called me so I could have apologized to the people who had come through with the largest turnout in the club's history.

Sam Gilbert advised me to fine Sidney $500. ''The only thing he understands,'' said Gilbert, ''is money. Fine him immediately.''

I called Sidney into the office the next day to explain that we took personal appearances very seriously in Portland. I told him he was a celebrity in our town now so his conduct off the court was as important as that on the court. I also told him that I didn't believe in fining players and that the few times I had ever done so, I had always found an excuse to give the money back.

I just don't believe in taking a player's money away from him. In this case, however, I told Sidney I was going to fine him $100 and send the check to the Clark College Booster Club, which had sponsored the dinner. I wish now that I had listened to Gilbert's advice.

Backtracking a bit, we made a couple of mistakes during the off season and then ran into one piece of incredibly bad luck. First we sold Leroy Ellis to the Los Angeles Lakers, and then we traded Jim Barnett to San Francisco for some draft choices. Both of these moves were criticized at the time, since these players were two of the team's top three scorers the previous season. The Barnett trade eventually enabled us to acquire some good players. But selling Ellis was a disaster. We did so at Todd's insistence, he kept telling us how Leroy "died" on the road. I approved the trade reluctantly but only because a third-round draft choice named Bill Smith, a 7' center from Syracuse, had looked very good in our rookie camp. He also played extremely well during the early part of the season so it looked like we had made a real steal in the draft. Unfortunately, just as Smith was beginning to come into his own, he collided with Mel Counts of Phoenix and wrecked his knee, an injury which ended his career. I insist to this day that, had Smith not been injured, the deal would have come out looking very good.

Adelman, Gregor, Knight, McKenzie, Petrie and Schlueter were hold-overs. We acquired Jim Marsh from USC as a free agent and picked up Willie McCarter from the Lakers; Darrell Imhoff, a veteran center, joined the team after Smith's injury. Beside Wicks, three players from the draft made the team. They were Charlie Yelverton of Fordham (second-round), Larry Steele from Kentucky (third-round), who is now the oldest Blazer in point of service, and Bill Smith.

The club went to pot. The season started badly. Petrie required knee surgery just before the first exhibition game and could only play 60 games during the season, never at top speed. From there things got worse. By mid-season, Wicks and Petrie, expected to form one of the most explosive offensive teams in the league, were feuding in the press and on the radio. I think each considered himself a threat to the other and it was reflected both on and off the court.

The blowup came at a game in Chicago between Christmas and New Year's. After the game Wicks was interviewed on a post-game show in which he said, "We stink," and criticized both his teammates and the coach. I was in Hawaii on vacation at the time and called Todd. He said he would handle the situation at the next practice; but, instead of returning to Portland and immediately coming to grips with the problem, which I thought was the responsibility of the coach, he elected to return via Las Vegas, where he wanted to spend New Year's Eve.

I knew I would have to replace Rolland, but I was hoping somehow to tough out the season. Things went from bad to worse and in February I called Rolland in and told him I was going to make a change. Stu replaced him on an interim basis and somehow we struggled through the season, winning only 18 games.

It was typical of the season, but in the last home game we routed the New York Knicks, 133-86. In the next game in Phoenix we were blown out by the incredible score of 160-128.

Despite the miseries, attendance increased to 6,988, up from 6,135 a game the first season. Only two crowds were smaller than 5,000, compared with 15 during our first campaign.

If the 1970 college draft was the best in the history of the NBA, the 1972 draft was to prove the worst. The only player from the draft who became a genuine star talent was Bob McAdoo. We won the coin flip that year and had the right to the first selection. We planned to select McAdoo. We invited him and his agent, Al Ross, to Portland, and they arrived with a large entourage. We met them with an equally large group including Tonkon; Terry Baker, the former Heisman trophy winner who is one of our lawyers; Sarkowsky's personal attorney, Irwin Treiger; and myself. The meeting lasted from 7 p.m. to 5 a.m. the following morning. When it finally broke up, we shook hands on a deal and agreed to get a couple hours of sleep before returning to the office at 9 a.m., at which time the lawyers would draw up the contract which McAdoo would sign.

When I returned in the morning, Ross told me that McAdoo had changed his mind. He insisted on his initial set of demands, which were astronomical and totally out of line. I called Herman, who had returned to Seattle, to report this development. He said, "Tell them to go to hell." So I sent them back to Los Angeles.

That is the story of how the Trail Blazers did not draft McAdoo.

There would have been some serious problems even had we elected to. During his junior year, he had signed a contract with the Virginia team of the ABA while still a minor. There was no assurance—and, in fact, serious doubt—that we could break the contract. So we decided to forget the whole thing and instead picked LaRue Martin of Loyola in Chicago. It turned out to be an enormous mistake, but if you look at the other players in that year's draft, none of them have ever cut up any fancy touches in the NBA.

The draft that year was one of the strangest in our history. LaRue was one of the nicest kids ever to play for Portland, but he never fulfilled his promise as a player. Our second-round choice was forward Bob Davis from Weber State. We will never know. He showed up with a bad knee and saw only 41 minutes of action in nine games. We had two choices in the second round and used the other to select guard Dave Twardzik of Old Dominion. I made a trip to New York to try to sign both Davis and Twardzik. Davis was represented by Lew Schaffel and Jerry Davis; Twardzik was represented by Norman Blass and Chuck Kaufman, with whom we had dealt when we signed Petrie.

I met with the Davis contingent first. We agreed to terms and I questioned them about the condition of his knee. We had previously been assured by the coach at Weber State that he had only missed a couple of practices and it was nothing serious. The agents assured me of the same thing. When Davis arrived in Portland, our doctors, after examining him, operated the following day. We later renounced the contract. The matter went to arbitration and was one of the few times a club won an arbitration decision in a dispute with a player.

Next came Twardzik with Kaufman and Blass. We agreed to the salary and bonus immediately but ran into a snag on the length of a no-cut contract. I didn't want to commit for more than one year but they insisted on two years. We didn't sign Twardzik so he signed with the Virginia Squires of the ABA instead. I now regret that it wasn't the other way around and we had signed Twardzik instead of Davis. Our fourth choice was Ollie Johnson of Temple, who has had a career as a good journeyman in the NBA. And our fifth choice in the third round was a beauty, center-forward Lloyd Neal of Tennessee State, who is still doing his thing. Neal beat out Martin for the job at center, averaged 13.4 points a game, hauled in what is still a club record 967 rebounds and was runnerup to McAdoo in the balloting for Rookie-of-the-Year honors.

We chose Jack McCloskey of Wake Forest as the coach to replace Todd. I was impressed with his intensity, his desire to coach in the NBA and the great recommendations I received. Everyone in basketball was in his corner, among them Eddie Gottlieb and Harry Litwack, the dean of college basketball coaches who was closing out a long career at Temple. Jack had the reputation of being tough, a quality I was convinced we needed to develop some discipline on the team. He also had the reputation of being excellent with the media.

McCloskey kept only four holdovers from the 1971-72 team—Petrie, Wicks, Adelman and Steele. We added pros Charlie Davis, obtained from Cleveland; Greg Smith from Houston; Terry Dischinger from the Detroit Pistons; and, for a short time, Dave Wohl.

The Blazers improved, winning 21 and losing 61. But they got off to a 1-11 start and posted the worst home record in history with only 13 wins. Petrie (24.9 points a game) and Wicks (23.8 points a game) did their thing offensively, but it wasn't enough to climb out of the cellar. However, attendance continued to improve with an average of 8,134 a game.

In 1973 no player available in the college draft was to join the Trail Blazers. Our first-round pick, Barry Parkhill of

Virginia, and fourth-round selection, Bert Averitt from Pepperdine did not sign and we had traded our second and third-round selections. At the time, at least, we didn't care. In a trade of first-round draft choices with Cleveland, we obtained veteran forward John Johnson and veteran center Rick Roberson for letting Cleveland have the right to pick Jim Brewer. McCloskey was high on both players and the media almost unanimously applauded the move.

Conducting the 1973 college draft—Glickman and Stu Inman, Director of Player Personnel.

There were seven holdovers that season—Petrie, Wicks, Steele, Neal, Ollie Johnson, Martin and Greg Smith. Bernie Fryer joined the team as a free agent after a widely publicized letter-writing campaign to sell himself. Dennis Layton, Bob Verga and Mark Sibley were with us for varying periods.

Things started well. Season ticket sales were up to 2,971.

In the opening game, the Blazers were awesome in blasting the Capital Bullets, 132-87. We won our first three and after 42 games we held a respectable record of 19 wins and 23 losses. We seemed to be on our way to our best year.

Petrie was named to start in the All-Star game. He was averaging 25.6 points a game (fifth in the NBA), was in the top ten in foul shooting and was shooting .490 from the floor. Wicks also played in the All-Star game in Seattle and played well.

Two days later we started our annual January road trip, the toughest of the season. We are always out of our building for three weeks in January. In Atlanta, Petrie twisted an ankle which took a month to heal. During that road trip we lost four of our starters for varying periods of time. The home record was a respectable 22-19 but we were terrible on the road—5-34—plus we suffered two losses on neutral courts. At one point we lost 21 consecutive road games, still a club record.

We finished in last place and had the dubious distinction of flipping the coin once again for the first selection in the college draft, now with Philadelphia. But this time it meant something. We were hooked into a conference call while the flip took place at a league meeting in Los Angeles. Irv Kosloff of Philadelphia was designated by Kennedy to make the call on the flip; he called ''heads'' and it turned out ''tails.'' When it was announced to me, as the press gathered in our office, I became so excited I dropped the telephone. The reason was obvious. We had won the right to select Bill Walton in the college draft!

At UCLA, Walton had set an all-time career shooting mark, had broke Kareem Abdul-Jabbar's all-time rebounding record, and had been second only to Jabbar in scoring. His teams won a record 88 straight games and two out of three national championships. Obviously, Walton was the Moses who was going to lead the Trail Blazers to the promised land.

As we reviewed our situation at the end of the season, we gave thought to the possibility of a coaching change. I was opposed to making such a change, as I thought McCloskey and his assistant, Neil Johnston, deserved a shot now that we had Walton. I must confess that, in retrospect, I was probably wrong. I thought our problem was not in the coaching but in some of the players, and thought we should give consideration to getting rid of Wicks. That suggestion, however, was rebuffed by our owners. They insisted that Sidney's problem was coaching. On this issue I turned out to be right.

At any rate, Sarkowsky informed us that he intended to exercise an owner's prerogative to make a change. His choice was Lenny Wilkens, then finishing an illustrious career in the NBA with Cleveland. Lenny had been player/coach in Seattle and had become a friend of Herman's. Firing McCloskey was one of the toughest things I have ever had to do, because I was genuinely fond of McCloskey as a person and thought then—and still do—that he was a good basketball coach.

With the acquisition of Walton, the sale of season tickets rocketed to 6,218, but our problems, instead of ending, were just beginning.

Injuries limited Bill to just 35 games and he wasn't healthy in all of those. He showed his potential early. After 13 games he was leading the NBA in rebounding and blocked shots, was shooting .515 and averaging 16.8 a contest.

He had had a history of knee problems throughout his career at UCLA, and when he reported to Portland he underwent knee surgery immediately. Bill had decided to build a large A-frame house on the banks of the Willamette River, and rented an old home in Sellwood while it was being constructed; but the building was delayed, cold weather set in, and all of this added to the problems of a youngster who was used to roaming the California beaches in shorts.

One thing after another happened. The owners thought it would be a good idea to bring Sam Gilbert, who then represented Walton, to Portland for a meeting. It turned out to be a big mistake.

At the time Walton had as permanent house guests Jack Scott and his wife. Scott had become a controversial figure as Director of Athletics at Oberlin College and as an author of sports books. He accompanied Bill to the meeting with our owners Weinberg and Sarkowsky. Ralph Shapiro, Bill's attorney, was also there.

As I understand it, Walton and Scott had never met before Bill signed to play with the Trail Blazers and moved to Portland. But because of their mutual interest in sports and their similar outlook on sports and politics, they had started corresponding while Bill was still at UCLA.

When Walton moved to Portland he invited Scott to visit him. He has been here ever since. Jack and his wife Micki shared a home with Bill and Susan until recently when the Scotts became parents and purchased a home of their own.

Scott has had an interesting career as a high school and college athlete, author, instructor at the University of California and Athletic Director at Oberlin College. He is invariably described in the press as "sports activist" Jack Scott. What the hell is a sports activist? Damned if I know.

I do know that Scott holds some outspoken and controversial opinions about sports that popular nellyism would insist on calling radical. Many of them aren't so radical, and Jack and I would find ourselves in total agreement. On other issues we would be diametrically opposed.

For example, Jack is passionately and vehemently opposed to the use of pain-killing drugs which permit an athlete to play at the risk of permanent physical injury. So am I.

We have one rule on the Trail Blazers. Players are never to use any drugs or pills other than an aspirin tablet without the specific authorization of the team doctor.

"Playing hurt" is supposed to be some kind of badge of honor in sports. Yes, athletes have to learn to live and play with some degree of pain, but only the player himself can make that decision. A doctor can diagnose an injury, for example, as a slightly sprained ankle, but he can't look inside the ankle and determine how much it hurts.

I tell our players that anyone who plays "hurt" at the risk of permanent injury is a fool. It's not entirely altruistic—he's also damaging the team. But if there's no risk of further injury, even if it means playing with some pain, he's expected to play. As our former team doctor said, "It can hurt you but you can't hurt it.'' Jack also believes players should have a voice in the selection of a team doctor. I can't fight that one, either, although I seriously doubt they would take the time and trouble to research and investigate the selection as we do.

Jack is opposed to artificial playing surfaces—another issue on which we agree. We rarely even practice on a tartan playing floor. If the rash of injuries to running backs and quarterbacks is even remotely caused by artificial turfs — and there is evidence that it is—then the National Football League is crazy not to outlaw them immediately.

On some issues, however, Jack and I would never agree. He points with pride to the fact that when he became Athletic Director at Oberlin the first thing he did was to discontinue charging admission to sports events. He believes the Athletic Department should be funded just like the Physics Department.

I believe the athlete should be treated the same way as any other student, but this is the real world. If thousands of people want to watch the football team perform, I see nothing wrong with charging them for the privilege.

In all the controversy surrounding Walton, Jack acquired the image of being his ''Rasputin,'' maneuvering Bill for his own purposes.

I never believed it. Bill has a mind and mouth of his own. What was mostly overlooked in most of the controversy is that it's rather difficult to play basketball in the NBA when you suffer nine broken bones in one year.

Now back to the meeting, which I could not attend due to an Eastern road trip. Gilbert told our owners, and later the press, that Bill was seriously considering giving up basketball, that he was unhappy with his teammates and coaches in Portland, didn't like the city, etc. Bill later denied saying any such thing, but disillusionment set in.

Shortly thereafter, the famous incident involving Patty Hearst developed. It was alleged in a newspaper article that the Scotts had rented a farm house in which they harbored Patty

Hearst while she was a fugitive from justice. The whole thing was blown out of proportion by the media. It took a ridiculous amount of my time just to deal with the sports writers and radio and television newscasters. The whole episode helped demoralize the club. When the story broke, I was up all night in New York answering phone calls from newspapers and radio stations all over the country, then joined the club on a flight to Boston. When we arrived at the hotel, I went to bed for the first time in 24 hours and got up about 5 o'clock. I was going down to the lobby to accompany the team to Boston Gardens when I was confronted by a couple of newspapermen from a Boston paper. They said they wanted to confirm a story that Bill Walton had driven Patty Hearst across the country to a farm house in Pennsylvania.

"Look," I said, "Bill Walton could shave his beard and could trim his hair, but he can't stop being seven feet tall. You tell me you seriously believe he could drive Patty Hearst clear across the country and no one would have spotted him?" That's an example of how ridiculous the thing became.

However, on the court we boasted our best record with 38 wins. The home record of 28 wins was also our best. For the first time, Portland climbed out of the Pacific Division cellar—into third place. And for the first time we played a good defense, holding opponents to fewer than 100 points 34 times. That had happened only 23 times in the first four seasons combined.

We had needed a playmaking guard, a problem solved by "unretiring" Lenny Wilkens when he obtained his playing rights from Cleveland. So Coach Wilkens played himself as our third guard and did a fine job.

A 10-31 road record plus, of course, Walton's injuries, prevented us from reaching our goal of making the playoffs. Still, we came close and there was optimism for the year ahead.

Just when things were calming down, the famous press conference in San Francisco occurred—Bill joined with the Scotts in issuing a statement in which, among other things, he said,

"In closing, I would like to reiterate my solidarity with Micki and Jack and also to urge the people of the world to stand with us in our rejection of the United States government."

That's what he said. No sense denying it or claiming that he was misquoted. It's on tape and on film.

What was not quoted was the following excerpt from the same statement: "The sooner *the present government* of the United States is forced to stop trying to eliminate progressive cultures, the human race will be in a much better position to achieve the potential greatness it possesses." The italics are mine, not Bill's.

In a later, clarifying statement he said the following: "Our statements issued in Glide Memorial Church on April 9 indicate that given the recent actions and policies of the United States government and their agencies, we feel that we, as a non-violent, peace-loving people, have a moral obligation to disassociate ourselves from the present administration made up of Ford, Rockefeller and Kissinger (none of whom was duly elected).

"It is important that I stress the love that we have for the American people. It is this specific administration and its immediate predecessors that we don't want anything to do with."

As events subsequently unfolded, not too many Democrats could disagree with that. Neither, for that matter, can I.

Mail poured in like an avalanche and the phone rang off the hook. The vast majority of the letters came from outside the state of Oregon and it is my guess that a substantial number of them were from members of the John Birch Society.

If the media had quoted Bill's statement in its entirety, or if the clarifying statement containing the words "the present administration" had been used in the first place, the Democrats, at least, would have applauded his remarks.

It didn't happen that way, however, and it caused quite a commotion. We had calls from season ticket holders threatening to cancel their orders unless we got rid of "that lousy Commie"; but in all, we lost a grand total of eight seats. The only time I got angry was when they opposed his right of free speech. A couple of callers didn't even have the courage of their convictions. They cancelled the seats in their company name but renewed them personally.

The club issued a statement in response to what Bill had said. I told the letter writers that I approved of his right of free speech, even if I didn't approve of everything he said. In all, we answered more than 1,000 pieces of correspondence.

In time, the whole incident cooled down.

For our second season under Wilkens we stayed with eight holdovers— Wicks, Petrie, Walton, Neal, Steele, Clemens, Anderson and, for his last season, LaRue Martin. We added new pros Steve Hawes, a fine backup center from the University of Washington, and Steve Jones, former star at Franklin High of Portland and the University of, Oregon who had played in the ABA. The draft of 1975 was to prove significant. Our first-round choice was guard Lionel Hollins from Arizona State and the second was a little-known forward from Long Beach State, Bob Gross. Despite the optimism of the year before, the team got off to a slow start, losing the first four and five of the first six. During the first three months the club won 12 and lost 21. We came back to post a 25-24 record from January through April, but it wasn't enough. Portland finished last again in the Pacific Division with 37 victories. The team was still floundering.

In the meantime, Larry Weinberg had taken over ownership control from Herm Sarkowsky. Herm had become involved with the new NFL football team in Seattle and Pete Rozelle frowns on his owners being involved in sports other than football. Herman took a minority position by selling his stock to Weinberg. The two of them had previously bought out Bob Schmertz when Bob became so engrossed with basketball that he purchased the Boston Celtics. (He was to live to see them win an NBA championship before his untimely death.)

All during the season Larry assessed the team and the coaching. We reviewed Lenny's strengths and his weaknesses and decided to make a change only if certain people were available. Our shopping list included only four coaches. Paul Snyder of Buffalo solved the problem for us when he decided to fire Jack Ramsay after Jack had compiled a tremendous record and had taken the Braves to the playoffs two straight years. After two interviews we signed him to a contract. That was the first of several important developments which would set the stage for the following season, when the Trail Blazers were to go all the way to the NBA championship.

Announcing the selection of Jack Ramsay as Coach of the Trail Blazers.

BLAZERMANIA

CHAPTER VIII

IF you work hard enough, scheme long enough—and get a little lucky—suddenly everything falls into place. That's what happened to the Portland Trail Blazers in 1976-77.

After six years of frustration, misfortune and—let's face facts, some mistakes on our part—we put it together and won it all. Sports writers referred to our fans as "long-suffering," but I take issue with the description. Seven years is a relatively short period of time in the history of any sports franchise. It took the New York Knicks, with every conceivable advantage any organization could wish to have, twenty-four years to win their first championship. We did it in seven.

When we were making application to the NBA, it was reported to me that Ned Irish, President of the Knicks and of Madison Square Garden, asked a league meeting, "How am I going to put the name Portland on the marquee of Madison Square Garden?" I hope the present operators of the Knicks will be pleased to put our name there now.

The first good thing that happened was the signing of Jack Ramsay as our new coach. For the decision to sign him, credit goes to Stu Inman and Larry Weinberg. The fact that he was available in the first place was pure accident—Paul Snyder had unexpectedly decided to fire him in Buffalo in spite of the fact that he had compiled an excellent record there.

The next good thing was Ramsay's selection of Jack McKinney as his assistant coach. Coaching is a lonely job and a good assistant is important to the operation. It gives the head coach someone to talk to. But McKinney is more than that. He is a good scout, and good at helping Ramsay design tactics and strategy; he also helps our cause by preventing Ramsay from getting kicked out of games for technical fouls.

The third good thing was something we literally didn't want to happen—we were unable to sign Geoff Petrie to a new contract. We had been negotiating with Petrie and his agent, Larry Fleisher, for the better part of a year, but we finally reached an impasse.

When it later became necessary to trade in order to obtain Atlanta's pick in the Dispersal Draft, the fact that we couldn't sign Petrie made it more palatable to involve him in the trade.

Good fortune struck a fourth time with the signing of Dave Twardzik, whom we had originally selected as a second-round draft choice but who had elected to play in the ABA. Dave was available because Virginia had neglected to perform under his contract and his agent had therefore declared him a free agent. We had been following Twardzik's career carefully in the ABA, so when he became available we signed him immediately.

Three events of historic importance to the NBA happened simultaneously—the settlement of the Robertson lawsuit; the signing of a new Collective Bargaining Agreement with the Players Association; and the expansion of the league with the addition of four teams from the American Basketball Association.

The Robertson lawsuit was an anti-trust action filed by the Players Association. It derived its name from the fact that Oscar Robertson was President of the Players Association. It sought to outlaw the draft, the Option Clause in contracts and the Compensation Rule which required a team acquiring a player who had finished his contract and signed with a new team to compensate the team which had lost his services.

The settlement of the lawsuit in the new Collective Bargaining Agreement legalized the draft, eliminated the Option Clause in contracts except for one year for rookies, and phased out the Compensation Rule.

All this took place at our league meeting at Hyannisport in June of 1976. Much of the credit for these positive developments belongs to our Commissioner, Larry O'Brien, who brought them off within one year of being chosen for the job.

The advantages were immediately apparent. We got rid of a costly and time-consuming lawsuit which had cost us about a million dollars a year in legal fees. The collective bargaining agreement gave us a chance to level off the escalating salaries we were paying untested rookies. Although there will not be any substantial savings, at least most of the salary money will go to the players who have earned it by their performance on the court and not to unproved highly-touted college stars. Expansion brought to an end the bickering between two leagues and created one major league of professional basketball.

A fringe benefit of expansion was the decision to hold a Dispersal Draft of those ABA players not on the rosters of the four teams coming into our league—Denver, Indiana, the New York Nets and San Antonio. That draft enabled us to obtain Maurice Lucas.

When the details of the Dispersal Draft were agreed upon, Stu did a magnificent job of research. He held conversations with ABA coaches, college coaches, even high school coaches, other players and whomever he could find who could give him a scrap of information. The more research he did, the more it was apparent that Lucas was the player we wanted.

At first it looked like there was a good chance we could obtain Lucas with our own pick, which was number six. But as we continued our research and as the date of the draft drew near, it was obvious we were going to have to trade down to get him. It developed that we had to trade all the way down to Atlanta, which had the second pick. (We knew Chicago was going to take Artis Gilmore with the first pick.) Atlanta wanted Geoff Petrie, and we reluctantly agreed. Then they came back with the demand for another player. We finally agreed to give up both Petrie and Steve Hawes, a forward-center whom we liked as a backup for Walton. But if we were going to obtain Lucas, that was the price we had to pay; and we made the deal.

Having acquired that pick, we tried to trade our number six choice as a package including Sidney Wicks, hoping to obtain a replacement for Petrie at guard. The player we obviously were going to get was Moses Malone, an excellent prospect who had come into the ABA straight out of high school. But the other teams shied away from his purchase price of $350,000 plus an enormous salary. While the Commissioner was conducting the role call via conference telephone call, I was on the phone with Eddie Donovan of the Knicks trying to persuade him to take Malone. We wanted at least enough cash to pay for Lucas, who was earmarked at $300,000. We couldn't make a deal with the Knicks, so we went ahead and selected both Lucas and Malone in the draft.

We drafted Malone with no intention of keeping him for the Trail Blazers; we intended to involve him in a trade. I thought we could put together a package of Moses Malone and Sidney Wicks in a trade for a first-rate guard. However, we were not able to trade for any one of six on our list.

A few weeks later I telephoned Red Auerbach in Boston. In our usual needling way, I said, "You're the great Red Auerbach and I'm going to offer you a deal that you will turn down. Then I'm going to leak it to the Boston papers and expose you for the phony you are."

"What do you have in mind?" he hollered.

"I'm going to offer you Sidney Wicks and Moses Malone for Jo Jo White."

"At least you haven't insulted my intelligence," said Red. "I'll have to think about that one for awhile."

About a week later he called telling me I had offered him too good a deal, but he simply wasn't going to part with Jo Jo. "He has helped me win a couple of championships and I won't let him go."

"Red, when the time comes that we are as good as Boston," I told him, "I hope we prove as loyal to our people as you have proved to Jo Jo."

Unable to make a deal, we eventually purchased Herman Gilliam from Seattle in a straight cash transaction.

Ramsay didn't want any part of Malone, even in training camp, so all summer long we tried to make other deals for him. However, we weren't going to give him away.

Ramsay's objection was absolutely correct. With Walton playing at center, Maurice Lucas playing at strong forward, and Lloyd Neal as the backup for those two, Moses would have no playing time. Between center and power forward there are 96 minutes of playing time and he felt that Walton, Lucas and Neal could handle it adequately. (We were aware that Lloyd was going to have knee surgery but we did not know that his recuperation would take virtually the entire season. He wasn't the real Lloyd Neal until the playoffs, when he did play effectively and helped us win the championship.)

Finally, we brought Malone to camp and he looked terrible. He was a good kid and tried hard but he had difficulty mastering Ramsay's offense, which called for most of our plays to be initiated through the center instead of being played to the center. With a player such as Bill Walton, that type of offense can be run effectively.

He started improving through the exhibition season, and in the last pre-season game he turned in an outstanding performance. But by that time Larry Weinberg had given John Y. Brown of Buffalo an option on a deal and Buffalo exercised it the next day. We finally traded Malone to Buffalo for cash and a first draft choice. Strangely, about a week later Buffalo, in turn, traded him to Houston.

While Neal recuperated from surgery we had to have another big forward. We were fortunate again in getting Corky Calhoun on waivers from Los Angeles. I would rate Corky's acquisition for the waiver price of $1,000 as one of the biggest steals in recent NBA history. We obtained Corky strictly as a specialist for defensive purposes. One of the problems in having too many good players is that they are not happy sitting on the bench, which causes nothing but turmoil for the coaches. Corky was happy with his assignment, which Ramsay carefully explained to him, and when we did have to call on him, he performed well. He did an especially fine job defensively on Julius Erving in the final Philadelphia series.

So here's how the team shaped up as we started the season. Our holdovers were Bill Walton, Lloyd Neal, Bob Gross, Lionel Hollins and Larry Steele. We obtained Maurice Lucas in the Dispersal Draft and Dave Twardzik from the ABA, purchased Herman Gilliam from Seattle and picked up Corky Calhoun on waivers. We kept three rookies. Our first draft choice was Wally Walker of Virginia. Our second draft choice was a speedster from Dayton named Johnny Davis, and we added a backup center named Robin Jones, whom we acquired as a free agent after he played in Europe the year previously.

One of the things that immediately impressed me about Ramsay was his refusal to fall back on that old coaching cliche, "We're new to each other and it will take us a long time to learn to play with each other."

At the press conference when we announced his selection, Ramsay did not talk about the distant future. He said that he had inherited the best coaching opportunity in basketball and predicted that Portland would make the playoffs for the first time the very next season. I liked his forthrightness and his optimism.

All through training camp Ramsay continued to exude confidence and optimism. "This is my kind of team," he told the assembled writers. "These players can execute the type of game that I love to coach—a running game and a pressing defense. I think we're going to become a very fine team."

We won seven of our first eight games, the best start of all time. And, except for the 17 games Bill Walton missed with injuries, the Trail Blazers never really looked back. We finished in second place in the Pacific Division, first place Los Angeles winning 53 games, more than any team in the league.

The Trail Blazers set club records for the most victories in a season (49), for most home victories in a season (35), and for most victories on the road (14). The team proved awesome in blowouts. In games decided by more than 20 points, the

Blazers won 14 and lost only one. Portland finished with the third best offense in the league, 111.7 points a game.

Individually, Bill Walton led the NBA in both rebounds (14.4 a game) and blocked shots (3.25 a contest) to beat out Los Angeles' Kareem Abdul Jabbar in both departments. Walton also finished seventh in shooting accuracy at .528. Maurice Lucas was ninth in rebounds with 11.4 a game, and Lionel Hollins was seventh in steals with 2.18 a contest. Bob Gross was sixth in shooting accuracy with .529.

We set a new all-time attendance record of 499,302, an average of 12,178 a game. This was 98.1% of capacity in the 12,411-seat Memorial Coliseum.

I can't tell you at what point in the season it happened or which sports writer coined the word, but about midway through the campaign the love affair between our fans and our players became known as "Blazermania." Ramsay encouraged the vocal support of the fans at every opportunity. Each succeeding game they became a little noisier and the standing ovations a little longer. They sensed that this might become a team and a year of destiny.

An omen of things to come occurred on November 5, early in the season, when the Trail Blazers literally demolished Philadelphia by a score of 146 to 104. It was the most awesome display of basketball I have ever seen. The Philadelphia players, collected by Fritz Dixon's millions, left the floor literally bewildered.

In my opinion, experience is the most important factor in any sport in playoff competition. I was concerned about our lack of experience. Only Herm Gilliam and Maurice Lucas had ever had any playoff experience and that wasn't much. I thought that if we could get past Chicago in the first round, we had an honest chance to win it all. Due to the playoff structure, we were to play the Bulls in a best-of-three series. I hate a three-game playoff series. Anything can happen. A single player may get hot, lead his team to two victories and it's all over.

As it turned out, our players gained enough playoff experience in the Chicago series to last a lifetime. It proved to be the toughest series on our way to the championship. The series' difficulties were compounded by the fact that the NBA referees had gone out on strike, so we were forced to use inexperienced officials through the early rounds.

Ramsay's concept of team play was particularly evident in our first game with Chicago on April 12, 1977. The Bulls came into the playoffs as the hottest team in the NBA. Coach Ed Badger had taken a club from early season reverses to the playoffs with an incredible second-half rush. We knew it was going to be a tough series. In the first game, Portland's team play was evidenced by 28 assists to 13 for the Bulls. The Bulls contributed 31 turnovers to help our cause. Lucas hit on 14 of 17 from the floor and Bob Gross on 7 of 10 to pace our first victory in Portland.

The second game was played in Chicago on Friday night, April 15, and it was a wire-to-wire thriller. Herm Gilliam was ejected in a fracas and Lionel Hollins and Dave Twardzik both fouled out, leaving us mighty weak at guard. But Portland stayed close right to the end despite a Chicago stadium wracking with more than 20,000 fans. Our starting lineup drew 27 of a possible 30 fouls as we were whistled for 33 personals to 18 for the Bulls.

It looked as if we were going to blow Chicago out early in the deciding game in Portland Sunday, April 17. We took a 55 to 46 halftime lead, but Chicago didn't quit. Bob Gross hit on 10 of 17 from the field and 6 of 6 from the foul line in exploding for 26 points, and Bill Walton contributed another outstanding game with 17 points, 11 rebounds and 4 assists before fouling out. Maurice Lucas scored 21 points before fouling out and Dave Twardzik hit 6 of 7 from the field and piled up 14 points before he fouled out. Mickey Johnson sizzled for the Bulls with a total of 34 points and 14 rebounds and John Mengelt was outstanding as they made a run at us in the second half. However, the Trail Blazers prevailed and reached the Western Conference semi-finals with a 106 to 98 victory.

Our opponent in the next round was the Denver Nuggets, with whom we had split during the regular season, each team winning once at home and once on the road. Because they had finished with the better record, Denver had the home court advantage, so the first game was scheduled there on April 20.

In retrospect, the series may have been won with 11 seconds to play in the first game when Maurice Lucas popped in a turnaround 14-footer and earned Portland the series-opening victory by a score of 101 to 100. It climaxed a strong game for Lucas, who had 23 points and 13 rebounds. Walton had 22 points and 12 rebounds and Gross contributed 18 points and 12 rebounds.

Dan Issel exploded for 36 points to lead Denver to a 121 to 110 victory in the second game on Friday, April 22, which squared the series. Issel hit on 11 of 19 from the field and 14 of 15 from the foul line, going to the free throw line himself the same number of times as the entire Portland team. Denver had 39 free throw chances to 15 for the Blazers. We had four more field goals than Denver and lost despite a staggering .598 shooting from the field.

Lucas turned in another outstanding effort with 29 points, nine rebounds, six assists and three blocked shots and Walton had 19 points, 16 rebounds, 10 assists and 7 blocked shots. Our 29 turnovers didn't help the cause.

The series returned to Portland for game three on Sunday, April 24. We took a 2-1 lead in the series with a 110 to 106 victory in a game that was tough all the way. David Thompson had one of his nights for Denver with 40 points. Lucas again led the way for Portland with 27 and Bill Walton had 26 as he hit on 12 of 21 shots.

In the fourth game, played on Thursday, April 26, Portland took a 3-1 lead but, again, it was tough. We led by only two points after three quarters, but pulled away in the final period for a 105-96 victory. Gross paced the Blazers with 25 points while Mac Calvin came off the bench for the Nuggets to score 28 points in just 21 minutes to keep Denver in the game.

Because an ice show was playing in the Denver building, the two teams were forced to take a layoff until Sunday, May 1, for game five. Denver won it, 114-105, in overtime. Portland had rallied with a 24-18 final quarter to force the overtime but then the Nuggets outscored Portland 13 to 4 to win easily. Thompson put on a 31-point show and Issel added 23. Hollins led the Blazers with 19 points.

The schedule forced us to play the next game in Portland the very next night, Monday, May 2, and we won the series with a 108-92 victory. The Blazers raced to a 33-16 first quarter lead and never looked back. Dave Twardzik had been injured in the previous Denver game, so Ramsay decided to give rookie guard Johnny Davis his first starting assignment in the playoffs. He responded with 25 points, hitting on 10 of 14 from the floor and 5 of 7 from the foul line, and also came up with 4 steals. Hollins contributed 21 points and 6 assists and Walton had 12 rebounds and 9 assists.

Blazermania was reaching a new crescendo as we prepared for the Conference finals against the Los Angeles Lakers, a team that had won the most victories in the league and which had defeated Portland in three of four contests during regular-season play. All the experts thought it would be an easy series for Los Angeles, some of them even predicting a Laker sweep.

Game one of the Conference finals was scheduled in Los Angeles on Friday, May 6. The Blazers burst to a 33-22 first quarter lead, made it 61-43 at the half and stayed tough for the victory. Four of our starters scored 20 or more points, 28 for Lucas, 25 for Hollins, 22 for Walton and 20 for Johnny Davis, the rookie turning in his second straight brilliant playoff game. Laker rookie Earl Tatum burned us with 32 points and Kareem was outstanding with 30.

Herm Gilliam, the guard we had purchased from Seattle, had had a somewhat erratic season; he was brilliant at times, inconsistent at other times. But the veteran guard was to make that deal look very good in the second playoff game at Los Angeles on Sunday, May 8. We had taken a 54-51 halftime lead, but the Lakers outscored us 26-16 in the third quarter and looked like a cinch to even the series. In the final quarter Gilliam poured in 14 points on every imaginable kind of shot. He finished with 24 for the game, hitting on 12 of 18 from the floor. It was probably Hollins' best playoff game as he hit for 31 points, highest single game total for the Blazers in the entire playoffs, and added 7 assists and 8 steals. Jabbar was brilliant for Los Angeles with 40 points, 17 rebounds and 3 blocked shots, but the Blazers returned to the friendly confines of Memorial Coliseum with a 2-0 lead over the Lakers.

The Blazers made it three-zip in the series in the next game on Tuesday, May 10, but it was tough. We took a 36-18 first quarter lead and it appeared as if the rest would be easy. But we scored only 37 points in the second and third quarters combined and the Lakers led by 2 points as we entered the final period. Portland came back for a 7-point final-quarter edge to win. It was a great battle of centers. Walton hit on 11 of 20 from the field to tie Lucas for scoring honors with 22 points, led the team in rebounds with 15 and assists with 9 and had 2 blocked shots. Jabbar again led the Lakers in scoring with 21 and also had 20 rebounds. For the second straight game Herm Gilliam was hot from the floor with 14 points on 6 for 9 shooting.

By now, the town was going berserk, as it looked like the Blazers had a chance to sweep the series from the Lakers. The fourth game was played on Friday night, May 13, and what a birthday present it was for me. The Blazers prevailed with a score of 105-101.

You have to give coach Jerry West and the Lakers credit. Down three games to nothing, they fought hard and almost moved the series back to Los Angeles. Jabbar was brilliant for the Lakers with 30 points, 17 rebounds and 4 blocked shots. Lucas led the Blazers with 26 points and 12 rebounds and Walton contributed 19 points, 14 rebounds, 6 assists and 3 blocked shots. Those types of stats were becoming almost routine for Walton as he prevailed in the series over Jabbar.

Now it was time for the championship finals against the Philadelphia 76ers. Television scheduling decreed that there would be a nine-day layoff before the series started in Philadelphia on Sunday, May 22.

The long layoff showed as Philadelphia captured the series opener 107-101. We were hurt by 34 turnovers which led to 26 Philadelphia points. We scored three more field goals than they did and out-rebounded the 76ers, but they were 27 for 32 at the line. Julius Erving scored 33 and Collins added 30 to pace the 76ers, while Lucas had 18 and Gross 16 for Portland.

Game two was played on Thursday, May 26 and the 76ers blew us out 107-89. It was our worst defeat in the entire playoffs, punctuated by a brawl between Darryl Dawkins and Lucas that threatened to erupt into a full-scale riot. Collins and Erving led the 76ers with 27 and 20 points, respectively, while Walton tried his best to retaliate with 17 points and 16 rebounds.

Ramsay warned that the series wasn't over and his team proceeded to back him up. Prior to the next game in Portland on Sunday, May 29, we held a brunch at the Coliseum for our radio and television sponsors. Larry and I each made a brief speech. I thanked them for their support over the years and told them, "This series isn't over yet." The team made Ramsay and me look like prophets. It was our turn to blow out the 76ers and we did it by a score of 129-107. We romped to a 34-21 first quarter lead, then blew out the 76ers with a 42-point final quarter. Lucas led the way with 27 points, while Walton followed with 20, 18 rebounds, 9 assists and 4 blocked shots. Another routine game for Bill.

In game four, played on Tuesday, May 31, the Blazers were simply awesome as they evened the championship series at two victories apiece with a 130-98 victory, the most decisive in the entire playoffs. In two consecutive games the Blazers had whipped the 76ers by a combined total of 54 points, perhaps the biggest two-game margin in NBA playoff history.

Portland sizzled to a 29-16 first quarter lead, then wrapped it up with a 41-21 third quarter. It was the second straight game in which the Blazers scored 40 or more points in a single quarter. Gross led Portland with 25 points and Lucas scored

24. Bill Walton scored only 12 points, but he added 13 rebounds, 7 assists and 4 blocked shots—another routine game.

The series moved back to Philadelphia for game five on Friday, June 3. This was the KEY game. We had to win a game in Philadelphia in order to win the championship, and now was the time to do it. The Blazers led 45-41 at the half, then exploded for a 40-25 third quarter advantage, the third straight game in which we scored 40 or more points in one quarter, and a slaughter seemed possible. But the 76ers fought back in the final quarter, 38-15, to make it a nerve-wracking ending. Gross led the scoring parade with 25 points in just 25 minutes of action; Walton hauled in a playoff career high of 24 rebounds and added 14 points. Lucas scored 20 and snared 13 rebounds, and Dave Twardzik, back in action, contributed 16 crucial points.

We chartered a plane to fly back to Portland immediately after the game, but most of us could have made the trip without the assistance of the engines. We were all sky high; we knew we could wrap up the world championship with a victory on our own court.

During the season, as we returned from each successive road trip more and more fans would be at the airport to greet the team. By the time of the playoffs, there was a crowd of several hundred people waiting after we won the second game in Los Angeles. Now, en route home, some of the players were kidding around and predicting how many fans would be on hand when we touched down at the airport at 4:30 in the morning. As I recall, the highest guess was 1,000.

When we alighted from that plane, I couldn't believe my eyes. The airport was wall-to-wall people. Police had to cordon off a narrow exit for the players to walk through while a crowd of more than 5,000 fans cheered them every step of the way. It was a sight and a moment never to be forgotten.

My own car had gone to the garage for repairs and I was using a loaned station wagon. It was pouring when I got out of the airport, and while thousands cheered, I walked around in the rain for almost two hours trying to find that car. When I finally did, I had to wait for another hour as the crowd cleared out of the airport. I finally got home about 8 in the morning. I hadn't slept all night and I couldn't sleep now. Excitement and tension about tomorrow's game kept growing. It was hard to comprehend—if the Blazers won that game, they would be the champions of the world.

The date was Sunday, June 5, 1977. The world's championship was on the line this sunny Sunday afternoon before 12,951 screaming, stomping fans, the largest crowd in our history. The teams were tied at 27-all after one quarter, but Portland turned in another 40-point performance in the second quarter and led by 12 at halftime. The 76ers cut the margin to 9 points at the end of the third quarter and weren't going to let it be easy. Hearts stopped all the way from section 1 to 86; only a last gasp miss from the floor by George McGinnis preserved the Portland victory. McGinnis had been no factor during the series but he snapped out of his slump with 28 points and 16 rebounds in the final game. Walton, however, responded with 20 points, 23 rebounds, 7 assists and 8 key blocked shots. Gross sizzled for the Blazers again with 24 points and Lionel Hollins contributed 20.

We were leading by two with 16 seconds to go when McGinnis forced a jump ball with Gross. The 76ers gained possession and had three attempts at the basket. One of them, by Lloyd Free, was blocked by Gross. Then McGinnis missed with five seconds to go. Walton didn't share the rebound, but he tapped it to Johnny Davis who scampered over the half line and threw the ball up as the game ended.

Walton tore off his jersey and threw it into the stands as the fans literally went berserk.

Then Blazermania really set in. What is Blazermania? I can't define it—I can only illustrate it.

Ratings for that final playoff game indicated that in Oregon we had a 96% share of the television audience. I am told that this is the largest share for any event in the history of television anywhere in the world.

The score clock at the moment the Blazers won the world
championship.

When the game was over, parades and dances started simultaneously in every neighborhood of Portland and in most of the cities in the state of Oregon.

That morning faithful churchgoers had left after the second hymn to get to the game on time.

Members of a symphonic band watched the game on television and forgot about their rehearsal.

There was a simultaneous honking of thousands of horns at the instant the championship game ended.

It was the biggest celebration since V-J day.

A woman fainted and, while being carried to an ambulance, still raised her finger to proclaim, "We're number one."

A policeman ended his radio transmission with, "Rip City radio, clear."

In the Washington Star a sports writer wrote: "It was like Washington when the Senators won the World Series in 1934 or Brooklyn when the Dodgers reached 'next year' in 1955 or the entire U.S. on V-J day."

In Prineville, fans parked campers overnight in front of a tavern to get good seats in front of the TV screen.

A Portland City Commissioner, Connie McCready, was a guest on a special run of an Amtrak train from Portland to Boise. She got off the train at Ontario, rented a hotel room, watched the game on television and then sped by automobile to catch up with the train in Idaho.

At the Crane Prairie Reservoir, Craig Ely of the Oregon Fish and Wildlife Department said, "Nobody would go fishing until the game was over."

All 22 prisoners cheered the Blazers in front of the television in the Deschutes County Jail.

Golf professional Jerry Mowlds took a portable television set with him while playing the final round of the Payless Classic pro-amateur tournament. He was even par until the basketball game was over, then finished with a 5-under 67.

Blazermania was pilots on flights broadcasting championship game bulletins to passengers.

At Geneva's Restaurant, a hangout for some of our players and fans, a dance started in the streets and lasted until the following day.

A baccalaureate speaker at Sandy Union High School interrupted his speech to give Blazer scores.

At commencement ceremonies at Oregon State University, virtually every other candidate for a degree listened to the game on a transistor radio.

Blazermania struck a minister at a church in Lake Oswego, who gave the shortest sermon on record and wrapped it up by offering a prayer for a Blazer victory.

Blazermania was fans plunging fully clothed into the Coliseum fountain after the championship game.

Gambling at a card parlor across the river in Vancouver, Washington came to a complete halt as the poker players watched the game on television.

The Oregonian wrote, "It was like the fall of Rome, the opening of the West and the discovery of atomic power at Memorial Coliseum Sunday."

Thousands of posters and T-shirts emblazoned with "Rip City," "We're No. 1," and "Red Hot and Rollin' " were sold outside Memorial Coliseum immediately after the game.

I'll tell you what Blazermania was. It was a love affair between a team and its fans, an entire city and state.

When the game was over, Commissioner Larry O'Brien presented the championship trophy, an event which CBS chose not to cover. That didn't dampen the enthusiasm. The trophy was prsented to coach Jack Ramsay and owner Larry Weinberg, but Ramsay insisted that all 12 players be on hand and share in the ceremony. It had been a team effort, and all were entitled to bask in this once-in-a-lifetime moment.

That night we had a private victory celebration. In the gathering were the players and their wives; all the members of our staff and their families; members of the media and a few other invited guests. I have never planned a celebration party. I still hold the superstitious belief that a manager should not plan for victory in advance. Larry's wife, Barbi, made the necessary arrangements.

The next day the city put a hastily-arranged parade together. There was a turnout of more than 250,000 people. It was total euphoria. The players and their wives and the coaches and their wives rode in the parade while all the members of the staff awaited them at Terry Schrunck Plaza across from City Hall. It was estimated that the parade would take one hour. It took almost three hours. Bill Walton and his wife Susan started the parade on their bicycles; they got about one block, then they had to pile into one of the convertibles provided for the members of the team.

The victory parade after winning NBA Championship with Jack Ramsay and Blazermaniacs.

Jack McKinney summed it up best when he said, "It was beautiful to see all those faces and every one of them was smiling."

It was a hot day as we sat there waiting for the players to arrive, and I had time to stop and think and to reflect about a lot of things.

I thought about my mother, now residing in Portland at the Robison Jewish Home for the Aged, and how proud she was. She had become a rabid Blazer fan.

Most important, my family was there to enjoy it. Our oldest daughter, Lynn, had been to the championship game but couldn't get a baby sitter so couldn't attend the parade. For my wife Joanne, my son Marshall and my daughter Jennifer it was one of the highlights of their lives. Marsh was born the year before we started the Buckaroos. He grew up with hockey and basketball, had been a ball boy and this year filmed our games on videotape for the coaches. Jennifer, 11, was one of our "stats" girls and became a Blazer fanatic. Jennifer was born prematurely the day following a football game I promoted between the San Francisco 49ers and Cleveland Browns. Their enjoyment of the NBA championship was as much a reward as one could hope for.

Our principal owners, Larry Weinberg and Herman Sarkowsky, were there with their wives to enjoy it all. Aside from their financial involvement, they had become familiar with all phases of our operation and had made invaluable contributions to our success. They, too, were entitled to this day.

I thought about Hurley and Salkeld and Saperstein and Reeves, now all dead, and how much they all had meant to me in reaching this day. I thought of other championships we had won in hockey. I thought of that first pro game which got me started as a sports promoter. I looked at George Rickles and Berlyn Hodges, who had been with me from day one. They understood.

Stu Inman had been primarily responsible for putting this club together. It was a team that consisted of nine draft choices, one free agent, one man claimed on waivers and one player purchased outright.

The other people on our staff were all there—my secretary, Sandy Sedillo, our bookkeeper Gail Miller, the girls in the ticket department, Mary Conchuratt and Meredith Wayt. I thought of the magnificent jobs done by our trainer, Ron Culp, and our team doctor, Bob Cook. There was our Promotion Director, Wally Scales, and our Publicity Director, John White, who could do more with a set of stats than any P.R. man in the business. They were all the unsung heroes of the championship. They were a wonderful staff. They were entitled to bask in the glory, which they did when the parade finally arrived.

There were several short speeches by notables. I gave a short talk and came up with what I thought was one of my best lines ever. During the final series, the Philadelphia writers had complained bitterly in their stories about Portland's weather, because it had rained quite a bit while the games were played in Portland. I reminded the crowd of their stories and said, ''I have a scoop for the Philadelphia media—it ain't raining on our parade today.'' It didn't get much of a laugh from that noisy crowd.

Larry Weinberg at the Schrunk Plaza celebration the day after the championship game.

Bill Walton at the Schrunk Plaza celebration the day after the championship game.

During the next week there were calls and letters literally by the hundreds from all over the country. The first wire I opened happened to be from Pete Rozelle. I heard from friends, relatives and acquaintances and so did all of our coaches and all the members of the staff. We were almost a month in responding to all of them.

There was one letter, however, that I had not received, and I was disappointed. I had not heard from former Commissioner Walter Kennedy. I had known Walter was sick, but I didn't realize how serious his most recent illness had become. About two weeks later I received a message from his secretary saying that Walter had dictated a letter just before he had gone to the hospital and had not had a chance to sign it. She thought I might like to have it. The letter read as follows:

June 8, 1977
Dear Harry:

Only you and I are left who can remember the horrors of hell you went through to get the financing the very night before the Portland franchise was granted in Los Angeles on that famous occasion. It seems like yesterday.

Harry, you above all others deserve great credit for Portland's winning the NBA title. Your patience and perseverence and creation of a great front office were the key elements in what ultimately was a victory on the court of play.

Without that other, there would be no team championship.

You have always been an outstanding guy and a great asset to the NBA and I am delighted beyond words that Portland won the title...I congratulate you with great sincerity and deep warmth.

Have a wonderful summer and bask in the glory!
Sincerely,
Walter Kennedy

Walter was never able to sign that letter before his untimely death, but I shall treasure it always.

We could—and I hope we will—win more championships. But for me and everyone else who experienced it, there will never be another pair of back-to-back days such as the Blazermania of June 5 and 6, 1977.

SPORTS AND THE TUBE

CHAPTER IX

NOW when I successfully change a light globe, my family considers it a monumental achievement. Therefore, one can understand my fascination with this thing called "television." When I watch a sports event, I absolutely marvel at split-screens, slow motion and instant replay. Television has made incredible technical advances in the presentation of sports.

Sports and television are married to each other, for better or for worse. As with most marriages, however, it's not all smooth sailing.

Last spring, during the NBA playoffs, I made the decision not to permit the televising of those home games which were not scheduled for national release on the CBS network. That decision elicited the following response:

1. A group of fans informed me that my head would make a good target for shooting practice.
2. It tied up our switchboard to the exclusion of nearly all other calls.
3. An avalanche of letters, few of which agreed with my position.
4. The editorial derision of most of the media in the state of Oregon.

Ironically, the most vitriolic comments came from sports broadcasters and editorial commentators at television stations which have never bid for the rights to Trail Blazers games, because they don't have the courage to preempt network television schedules.

The only sane voice in the whole hulabaloo was that of George Pasero, sports editor of the Oregon Journal. George, one of the best sports columnists in the country, has the ability to keep things in perspective and he did so in this instance. Bombarded with telephone calls urging him to "get Glickman," he wrote a column which calmed things down and then proposed that we televise one home game of the Conference finals as appreciation to our fans. This is exactly what we decided to do. Over the years I have taken my lumps from George, probably less than I deserved, and I have been lauded by him, probably more than I deserve. But that column is one for which I shall forever be indebted.

That decision, which I do not regret and would make again, was based on my experience with television through the years dating back to my days as a press agent in boxing, when television almost literally destroyed the sport. At that time, television was just beginning to undertake major efforts with sports. Boxing became one of its first major experiments. The International Boxing Club had contracts with the networks for a series of fights on Wednesday and Friday nights. Remember the Pabst Blue Ribbon fights on Wednesdays and the Gillette Cavalcade of Sports on Fridays?

Television created millions of fight fans but caused the loss of a million cash customers and the fight game has never been the same since.

It destroyed the identity of the athletes in a surfeit of fights. Remember my "white trunk vs. black trunk" survey mentioned in the first chapter?

My first direct experience with sports television came when I was handling publicity for the annual Shriners Hospital All-Star Football Game, held in Portland each summer between graduated high school seniors from the Portland metropolitan area and from the rest of the state. The game was inaugurated in 1948, spearheaded by Earl Riley, former Mayor of Portland, and Rube Adams, the president of Meier & Frank. The games were drawing crowds in the neighborhood of 20,000; the funds raised were given to the Shriners Hospital for Crippled Children.

In 1952 a local television station approached Riley and Adams with a proposition to televise the Shrine game. Without consulting anyone, Riley and Adams agreed.

When I learned of this decision, I protested strongly. I told them I thought that decision would jeopardize all future Shrine games. Then I asked them how much money they were getting for the rights. They replied that they had given the game to television without any rights money. The station had agreed not to announce the telecast until an hour before game time and also promised to make appeals for contributions to the Shriners Hospital during time outs. Riley and Adams felt that many people would so appreciate the televising of the game that they would send checks for this worthwhile charity as a result of these appeals.

I told them again it was a tremendous mistake and that, in the future, no one would ever believe they were not going to televise the game. As for contributions to the hospital, not one single dime was sent in by the people who watched it on television. Enough said about the generosity of what Hurley used to call the "freeloaders." I don't think it an accident that attendance at the next several games declined dramatically.

1952 was also the year in which I promoted my first professional football game and attracted a capacity crowd to Multnomah Stadium. The following year I scheduled a rematch between the Los Angeles Rams and Chicago Cardinals. About a month before the game I was approached by a couple of executives from another local station requesting permission to televise the game. I told them I had no intention of putting the game on TV, as it should be obvious to them that doing so would hurt the gate. Their response was that they didn't think televising the game would hurt the gate at all and would only create interest for all future games. I said that the same game had drawn a capacity crowd the year before; it was an excellent game and I looked for another good crowd for the coming game. They replied that this game would be another easy sellout.

"In that case, you don't have a thing to worry about. I'll let you televise the game and you don't have to give me a dime for the right." They looked at me with bewildered expressions.

"All you have to do," I continued, "is to guarantee that every ticket will be sold. You make up the difference between the actual gate and the potential gate."

That was the last I ever saw of them and the last time I ever heard from anyone involved with television that showing an event live doesn't hurt the gate.

Then we got into hockey, and since some of the owners also owned a television station, I thought they would be eager for the rights to the Buckaroos' games and would help us promote our new sport in Portland by putting our road games on television. In the second year of operation they decided to televise the first game from San Francisco. To do so, they preempted the network program "Beverly Hillbillies." The next day they got some letters and phone calls protesting the removal of the scheduled program. That was the last time they ever made an effort to televise one of our games.

Every promoter who has ever tried to sell tickets and televise an event at the same time soon found that he was playing to empty seats.

A few years ago Congress enacted a law called the "Anti-Blackout" Rule. The legislation forced a home team to remove the blackout restriction in its home territory for any game which is (a) to be televised by a national network and (b) is sold out 72 hours in advance of the starting time. I think it is highly discriminatory because professional sports thereby achieved the unique distinction of becoming the only industry in America forced to give its merchandise away free, after it has sold a certain amount of it.

Television can be the greatest single ally sports has—if properly exploited. Here I'm not thinking only about the dollars television heaps upon us for the rights to televise our games. If you are dealing with a sport which you believe you can sell to the public, the fastest way to promote it is to put it on television. The promotional value of television is as important as the dollars for the rights. In using television, however, certain rules of common sense must apply:

1. You can't expect to sell tickets and give them away at the same time.
2. You can't over-expose the sport or a single team because the viewers will become bored.
3. Put your best on television. Don't put on garbage and save the best for something else. If you're going on TV, go with your best shot.

I contend that the operators of sports teams make it fairly easy for television. We deliver a ready-made attraction. There is no need for script writers or costly sets. We even provide and pay—and pay dearly—for the stars. All television has to do is bring the cameras and their own operating crew. The price, however, that television extracts in return for all this is sometimes too high. For example:

1. It is absolutely wrong for a baseball game between the Los Angeles Dodgers and the Philadelphia Phillies for the championship of the National League to be played in a driving rain storm—just because the network has scheduled it for a particular time on a specified day.
2. It is absolutely wrong for a World Series baseball game to be played in near zero weather in mid-October—as it was in Cincinnati last year—just because television wants it in prime time.
3. It is absolutely wrong for television to interrupt the normal flow of a hockey game under the phony pretense of repairing a hole in the ice because television wants a commercial at a particular time.
4. It is absolutely wrong to create artificial time-outs, as television has done in professional football, with a "two-minute warning to both benches." I contend that any coach with a staff of ten assistants who doesn't know how much time is left in a game should be fired from his job.
5. It is absolutely wrong for television to alter the natural schedule of championship playoff games to suit its convenience. National television should not be permitted to

tell the Portland Trail Blazers to start a championship playoff game at 10:30 on a Sunday morning.

On this last point I can speak by reason of very recent and very personal experience.

Under its contract with the National Basketball Association, CBS insists on having a game to televise each Sunday during the playoffs—a perfectly logical and reasonable position for CBS to take.

Our series with Chicago in the first round of the playoffs went the maximum number of three games, insuring a Sunday game for the final contest of the series.

Next came our series with Denver. In a best-of-seven series, the team with the best record—in this case Denver—gets the home court advantage for games one and two and for games five and seven if they are necessary.

First, CBS tried to alter this arrangement. Denver vehemently protested, a position I certainly would have taken if the Trail Blazers had finished with the better record. Then CBS decided it wouldn't need a Sunday game in our Denver series after all because they would broadcast a Sunday game in the Los Angeles vs. Golden State series. The schedule was arranged accordingly. Then CBS decided it wanted a doubleheader. A new schedule was worked out which called for us to play in Denver on a Sunday afternoon and again in Portland on a Monday night. This forced the Trail Blazers to do exactly what we didn't want to do—play Bill Walton, with his knee problems, in back-to-back games during the playoffs. The fact that Walton's presence might add millions of viewers and dramatically increase the ratings didn't dawn on those guys on Madison Avenue. Fortunately, the Trail Blazers won both games and the series.

Then came our series with Los Angeles. At the last minute, the boys on Madison Avenue figured out that a game involving the Lakers and Trail Blazers—Kareem Abdul Jabbar against Bill Walton—might elicit more than casual interest among the sports fans of the country. So they decided to put the Friday night game on television, but wanted the starting time changed—after the tickets had been sold and the time announced.

CBS had envisioned a playoff finals for the NBA championship between Philadelphia and Los Angeles, with Jabbar against Erving—real live, honest-to-goodness, six million-dollar men.

Logic, common sense, the players, the teams, the fans, *everything* dictated that the series between Portland and Philadelphia should open on Friday night, May 20. But CBS thought otherwise. The network wanted to be assured of at least two Sunday games during the final round, and so dictated that the first game of the series would not be played until Sunday, May 22. But that wasn't bad enough. The second game should have been played the following Tuesday night. Again, CBS had other plans; the second game was scheduled for Thursday night, May 26.

And so, the Trail Blazers at the peak of their game, had to take an enforced layoff of nine days to play the first game in the finals and then lay around four more days in Philadelphia before they could play game two. As some comedian once said, "The only thing worse than spending a day in Philadelphia is spending two days there."

To their everlasting credit, neither the players nor the coaches of the Trail Blazers offered the long layoff as an excuse for the two defeats in the first two games in Philadelphia, although anyone who knows anything about basketball knows it was an important factor.

Then came the crowning insult. After winning two games at home to tie the series, the Blazers won game five in Philadelphia to take a 3-2 advantage. Game six was scheduled in Portland on Sunday, June 5. CBS told the league we would start the game at 10:30 a.m. I told the league "No way!"—only that wasn't quite the language I used.

In my particular religion, we don't go to church on Sundays. But many basketball fans do go to church, and a 10:30 starting time, aside from its ridiculously inconvenient hour, was an insult to them. I refused to do it. I bluntly told Commissioner

O'Brien that if CBS insisted on a 10:30 starting time, they would be showing a Philadelphia intrasquad game, because the Blazers wouldn't be on the floor. I don't know what I would have done if push came to shove. However, I had two things going for me. First, I knew darn well there was no way they would declare the game a forfeit if we didn't show up and, secondly, I had O'Brien in my corner on this issue. It was finally agreed that the game would start in Portland at 12:30 p.m. The letters and calls of thanks from priests and ministers confirmed the support for my position.

The arrogance of some of the television people is not to be believed, because next came the final insult—to the Trail Blazers, the National Basketball Association, the game of basketball and the sports fans of the country. When the game was over and the Trail Blazers had captured the NBA championship, CBS switched to the Kemper Open Golf Tournament. They didn't televise the presentation of the championship trophy, a traditional feature of every championship sports event since television got into the act.

Castigated long and loud by my partners in the NBA when he made the CBS presentation at our annual meeting, even Barry Frank, the President of CBS sports, admitted it was lousy journalism and promised never to let it happen again.

I'm the last person in the world to scoff at the dollars television brings us, because it would be difficult for the Trail Blazers and most other teams in professional sports to survive without them. But in any conflict between the cash customers in the stands and the free customers in front of the tube, it's no contest. My loyalty is with the ticket-holding fans. Regardless of the dollars involved, it would be a sad day indeed if sports were to become studio presentations.

While television offers us the opportunity to exploit our games before literally millions of fans—and delivers checks for millions of dollars into our greedy little hands—there comes a time when the operators of sports franchises must say, "Enough—you can't run our industry."

Television dangles its dollars; television decrees; and we're supposed to bow three times to the East, and hang the welfare of the players and the interests of the ticket-buying fans who have made the games possible in the first place.

Television offers some interesting possibilities for the future. Cable television is in its infancy. For years we in sports have heard about the prospect of pay-as-you-watch television. It's supposed to be the bonanza that will drop millions of dollars into our coffers. There is also closed-circuit television, with which the Trail Blazers experimented successfully during the recent NBA season.

But regardless of what television holds in store for the future, to me there is nothing like being there. I get my kicks out of being part of a capacity crowd watching any type of sports event, whether I'm promoting it or not. And I know full well that sports are primarily designed for the interest and enthusiasm of fans who come to the stadiums and arenas to cheer for their favorite teams.

LABOR-MANAGEMENT RELATIONS

CHAPTER X

ALTHOUGH I can still feel the glow of the Blazermania which rewarded our efforts on the court and in the front office last year, I know that I can't afford to take our future success for granted—or, for that matter, the success of pro sports in general.

Professional sports have always supported a dynamic industry; but right now changes are taking place that could seriously affect their future as popular spectator events. I think these changes and the way we handle them will play a big part in determining what the future of sports will be.

There has literally been a revolution in the sports industry in just the eight years that the Trail Blazers have been in operation in the major leagues of professional sports. We have gone full cycle from Reserve Clause, Option Clause and Compensation Rule to what will become, in three years, total freedom of movement for players. The effect that this is going to have on fans buying tickets in our buildings or watching our games on television cannot be predicted, but it will be significant.

That professional sports require some type of orderly process for acquiring and retaining playing talent is beyond dispute. We must have rules which will enable us to equalize playing strength so that we can promote sports contests in which either team has an honest chance to win. If we don't, we're collecting money at the ticket tills under false pretenses.

How to go about doing this, while at the same time protecting the rights of players, is an issue that has cost millions of dollars in legal fees over the course of the past several years, has engendered animosity between labor and management and has caused escalation of salaries beyond economic reality.

In the NBA the issue was resolved in the summer of 1976 with the signing of a new Collective Bargaining Agreement. It remains to be seen whether it will allow owners to operate at a reasonable profit, fans to enjoy honest competition and players to benefit by freedom of movement.

The most ingenious system ever devised to equalize playing strength is the annual college draft, which was dreamed up and introduced in the National Football League in the 1930's by George Preston Marshall of the Washington Redskins and George Halas of the Chicago Bears. The draft is designed to give the bottom teams in the standings first crack at the best college players of the preceding year, theoretically giving them the opportunity to improve their won-lost records.

For this potential to be realized, however, the teams must make the correct selections in the draft and then sign the players.

To assess accurately the future professional ability of a college player is one of the most difficult jobs in sports. Many Heisman Trophy winners and college All-Americans have been busts in the pros, while many unsung players from unknown schools have made it big.

How will he develop physically? How much will he mature emotionally? Does he have mental and physical courage? What kind of player will he be three years from now? Can he handle pressure? These are the kinds of questions a scout has to ask himself—and answer. Computers can't do it for him. They are as important as how high he can jump or how fast he can run.

In a sport such as basketball, where one outstanding player can turn a club around almost by himself, the draft is of incredible importance. Kareem Abdul Jabbar was instrumental in taking the Milwaukee Bucks from an expansion team to the NBA championship in just three years. The acquisition of Bill Walton, together with other draft choices, enabled the Trail Blazers to win the NBA championship in seven years. These two examples represent the shortest periods of time on record for an expansion team to win it all. It took a little longer for the Dallas Cowboys in football and the Philadelphia Flyers in hockey.

So it is of utmost importance to maintain the legality of the college draft, and I believe it's just as important to the players and fans as it is to the owners. A player coming out of college and embarking on a pro career wants to think that sometime he, too, can be on a winner.

In the Collective Bargaining Agreement signed with the Players Association following the settlement of the Oscar Robertson lawsuit, the draft was recognized as a valid instrument for the future of pro basketball. It also enabled the NBA to add four teams from the ABA, to become one major league of professional basketball.

The NBA never had a Reserve Clause in its player contracts. The clause was, however, in force in baseball. The Reserve Clause gave the club which originally signed a player the rights to his services virtually in perpetuity. That it is in violation of anti-trust legislation is beyond dispute.

The Reserve Clause was challenged several times all the way to the Supreme Court, most recently in the famous Jesse Flood case. The Supreme Court said it was up to Congress to change the rules. Two years ago, when the baseball owners thought they were home free, for a time at least, the Reserve Clause came to an inglorious end when an arbitrator named Peter Seitz declared Andy Messersmith a free agent and immediately made instant millionaires out of some very average ball players.

In basketball, the Option Clause was incorporated in our contracts. This clause stated that if a player completed the stipulated term of his contract and the team and the player could not agree on a new contract, the club had an "option" on his services for one additional year. In the NBA, if a player was in his option year, he received the same salary and fringe benefits as he did for the last year of his contract. In the NFL, on the other hand, he took a 10% cut in pay.

I never thought the Option Clause was vital to professional sports. All the Option Clause really did was add an additional non-guaranteed year to a contract. If you sign a player for three years and want an option on his services, why not sign him for four years in the first place? In our recent agreement with the Players Association, the Option Clause was phased out and will no longer be a standard feature of our contracts. We can have them, but they must be negotiated individually and for a period of one year only. Its demise is of no particular significance.

In the NBA and NFL we have operated in the past with a Compensation Rule which became more commonly known as the "Rozelle Rule" after Pete awarded the San Francisco 49ers two first-round draft choices as compensation for the loss of a player named Dave Parks to the New Orleans Saints. In that case, there was no doubt that Pete over-compensated in an effort to discourage clubs from doing the same thing in the future.

The Compensation Rule was really not very complicated. It simply stated that when a club lost the services of a player because he had completed his contract and the club and player could not agree on a new one, the team which acquired him to "compensate" the team which lost him. Theoretically, it was designed to make the team which lost the player "whole;" the compensation could take the form of cash, draft choices, another player or any combination of the three. If the two teams couldn't agree on compensation, the Commissioner made a binding decision.

This rule will be phased out of the NBA in three years; dropping it could prove to be of extreme significance. Together with the draft, it helped equalize playing strength between teams.

In its place, our agreement provides for a "right of first refusal." No one can predict the ramifications of this rule, but it could lead to serious problems between the "have" and "have-not" clubs.

For example, if a player were to complete his contract with the Portland Trail Blazers and negotiate a new one with the New York Knicks, all we would have is the right to match the offer of the Knicks. If we do so, we get the player. If we don't, we lose the player and get nothing in return.

This will present an enormous problem to a club such as Portland. Even though we have been successful in filling our building to capacity, we still have to play against teams such as the Knicks and Lakers with our capacity of 12,666 against their capacity of almost 20,000 and the corresponding potential in gate receipts. That's tough competition.

And it goes beyond gate receipts. The Knicks, for example, negotiate a local radio and television contract in excess of a million dollars a year. Given the size of our market, we have a good radio and television contract in Portland, but it's nickels and dimes compared to those in the larger cities. They start the season a million dollars ahead of us before we even throw up the first ball.

It is to be hoped that common sense will prevail and that the large cities and wealthy owners will not run the smaller cities and less wealthy owners out of business when the new "right of first refusal" comes into operation.

We have two recent and noteworthy examples of what can happen when an owner decides to open his wallet to go after playing talent. In our league, the Philadelphia 76ers first signed George McGinnis to a rich contract, then paid roughly six million dollars to acquire and sign Julius Erving. The fact that their owner, Fritz Dixon, happened to be enormously wealthy and has a nagging desire to wear a championship ring makes it a little tough on the rest of us.

It's not that other players demand the same contract as Erving, but a player who's worth $75,000 but is earning $150,000 will contend he's worth half as much as Erving and demand $300,000. That's when it gets scary.

George Steinbrenner spent several million in loose cash last year and the New York Yankees rewarded him with a world championship. Personally, I don't see that there's much satisfaction in winning a pennant by merely signing a check.

Salaries in professional sports have escalated in recent years, with corresponding increases in ticket prices, beyond anything remotely resembling economic good sense. The reasons, primarily, are the formation of rival leagues with their attendant bidding wars for talent, and court decisions which have made some of the rules under which we operated outmoded.

In almost every instance where a city had the required facility and an investor willing to pay the entry fee for the franchise, a major league franchise has been awarded by way of expansion.

But some cities or potential investors didn't have the patience to wait their turn, or thought they could sneak in the back door by forming a rival league whose only intention was to force a merger with the established one.

Along came a guy named Gary Davidson to start up new leagues in first basketball and then hockey and football. He made sure to award himself a franchise and then sold it off for a tidy profit. He also awarded himself the job of running the leagues. All of them wound up in a sea of red ink and only the World Hockey League survives. It's in such shaky condition that it won't last another year unless there's a merger with the National Hockey League. And ironically enough, Davidson is no longer around to pay his share of the freight.

A former partner in the Trail Blazers, the late Bob Schmertz, unfortunately provides a good example of the problems which could and did arise. He first acquired the New England franchise in the World Hockey League and then grabbed the New York franchise in the World Football venture. I begged him not to go for the football deal, but Bob got caught up in the glamour of professional sports and took the gamble. It cost him more than two million dollars in less than two years.

Accompanying the insane bidding for untested rookies caused by the introduction of rival leagues, we saw the advent of player agents to represent the players in negotiating their contracts.

I have no objection to players using agents to negotiate contracts. Indeed, in most cases it is a wise move for them to do so. Many agents are reputable lawyers or accountants who not only negotiate contracts, but also guard the player's money and investments zealously. A 22-year old kid is not equipped to handle a million-dollar contract and good agents do an excellent job in protecting them.

There are some in the trade, however, who are nothing but leeches. After signing a player to a contract, they forget all about him and leave the player to his own devices for the most important part of the job, managing his money and paying his taxes.

Even good agents frequently negotiate for hours and hours and hours to no good purpose. I suspect they do so to impress their clients with how hard they're working on their behalf. We have struggled harder signing a couple of second-round draft choices than we did signing Bill Walton.

I believe the major leagues of professional sports should be permitted to prescribe certain standards and qualifications for agents and that they should be duly licensed before they are allowed to represent players in contract negotiations. I think the reputable agents should form an association, similar to a Bar Association, and establish rigid ethical standards to which their members must adhere. They should police their own association and get rid of the fast-buck artists who give their profession a bad name. Then maybe we can start conducting contract negotiations in a dignified and orderly manner, the same as other industries.

I also hold strong opinions about the representation of a player by an agent who also happens to be the head of the Players Association. I speak here of Alan Eagleson of the NHL Players Association and Larry Fleisher of the NBA Players Association. Not only are they in command of their respective Players Associations (and they do a good job, too), but they also individually represent a number of the best players in the game. I think it ethically indefensible that they are permitted to do this. For one thing, as leaders of their respective associations they have access to every player contract in the league. The other agents do not share this information. Even the teams in the NBA are not privy to this material except in coded and numbered player lists. Eagleson and Fleisher should have to choose—either they represent the Players Associations or they represent individual players. They shouldn't be able to do both.

I have always made it a policy not to announce player salaries or bonuses, for the simple reason that I don't think it's anyone's business except the parties involved. The press always speculates and the press has always been wrong in those instances where I was the party of the second part.

It's not that I'm ashamed of the contracts to which I've affixed my signature. It's just that I think it's a private matter between the player and his wife and between them and the Internal Revenue Service. I have never asked anyone, including members of the media, how much he earns. I only hope everyone earns enough to support his family.

I also intensely dislike conducting salary negotiations in public. Fans have a legitimate right to know whether a certain player is going to play the ensuing season and the media has a legitimate right to report such a development. But it must be kept in perspective. A player is never unsigned until the signing deadline has passed, which is the opening of training camp. It's at that time that a player is a legitimate holdout.

I'm also opposed to conducting salary negotiations in the newspapers. Contract negotiations should be conducted in the privacy of an office.

One year our best and highest-paid hockey player, Art Jones, decided to inform me that he was going to be "tough" in negotiating his new contract. Before we held even one preliminary discussion about it, he issued an ultimatum in the press, the headline of which read: "Pay Me or Trade Me."

Well, I had my pride too, and I didn't want to look cheap to the fans. Players with the Buckaroos were always paid fairly and even generously by Western Hockey League standards. Jones didn't get traded and he didn't get paid what he wanted, or even what I was prepared to offer him before the tirade in the press.

I can truthfully state that in seventeen years of operating sports teams no player has taken a cut in salary if he was with us the year before.

Players and their agents come armed with all sorts of scoring statistics. However, there are only two figures that interest me—where we finished in the standings and where we finished at the turnstiles. From that point of departure we can get down to business.

Sometimes contract negotiations can get to be amusing. I recall a hockey player named Eddie Panagabko, who had been assigned to us by Boston. For a time I tried to change the custom of signing players in training camp by trying to sign them during the summer. It met with little success.

In this case, however, I mailed Panagabko's contract to his home in Estevan. I never heard from him. He arrived at training camp, where I called him into the office.

"I sent you a contract, Eddie," I said, "and I never heard from you."

"The contract was okay," he said.

"Then why didn't you sign it?" I asked

"The only thing a player ever has to argue about is his contract," he said.

"So start arguing," I told him.

"No, there's nothing to argue about, I like the contract and I'll sign it right now."

Another story involves Connie Madigan, with whom I had tedious and time-consuming contract negotiations annually. I decided I wanted Madigan to sign a two-year contract because I didn't enjoy negotiating with him each year.

He would simply sit for a couple of hours, state his demands and refuse any sort of compromise. I offered Madigan what I thought was a fair contract. He came back with a counter-offer which I thought was far too high. I kept creeping up little by little until I got within $250 of what he wanted, but then I stubbornly refused to go a nickel more. I forget what the amount was, but let's call it $12,000 and say I was up to $11,750. He still wouldn't budge and wouldn't sign.

"Connie," I said, "if I offered you twenty thousand, you'd probably still say no."

"That's right," he said, "it's twelve or nothing."

"In that case, Connie my friend, it's going to be nothing because that's the last I'm going to move."

He eventually signed.

During the past several years, sports fans have been greeted with headlines such as:

"Players vote to strike."

"Owners vote to lock out players from training camp."

"Pay me or trade me."

There has been more news on the labor-management front than there has been over what's really important—who won the game and why.

Sports are unique in the annals of private enterprise. Whereas a department store might be able to drive another one out of business by offering better merchandise at a lower price, in sports we can't drive our competitors out of business.

On the contrary, we must do everything possible to keep them *in* business. We can't play against ourselves—we need opponents. So the team we're trying to kick hell out of on the playing floor is our partner off the floor.

This fact of life must be recognized in the legislative halls and the courts, by players and their agents, and by the owners themselves.

It is to be hoped that the new Collective Bargaining Agreement in the NBA will bring a halt to litigation and the demeaning of the game caused by washing our linen in public. We have to get on with the job of what's important in sports—trying to win games and championships.

HUSTLING THE TICKETS

CHAPTER XI

IN the quarter century that I have been promoting professional sports attractions, more than six million people have spent more than 20 million dollars to watch the games I have urged them to attend.

If you include other expenses incurred by the fans in attending games, such as hotels, gasoline, babysitters, food and beverages and clothes (you think they advertise what to wear at the games for nothing?), you can triple that figure. Very often the cheapest item involved in attending a sports event is the price of the ticket.

Although very little of that money has rubbed of on me, I consider it an awesome responsibility. No one sweats blood, prays harder or hopes more fervently that the fans will be entertained and enjoy the game than the promoter responsible for bringing it to them.

The old-fashioned caricature of a promoter—a fat guy with a bald head and a big cigar sticking out of his mouth, trying to rip the fans off—went out with high-buttoned shoes.

Only two times in my career as a promoter have I felt that the fans were cheated.

The first of these involved the closed-circuit telecast of the first fight between Floyd Patterson and Sonny Liston for the heavyweight championship of the world. Closed-circuit telecasts are notorious for poor advance box office sale. These events invariably produce a last-minute gate sale. We have never had a loser, but there were times the morning of the show when I gladly would have sold out for a small loss.

For the first Liston-Patterson fight, we had a tremendous advance and were looking forward to our best crowd and best gate ever. About 1:30 on the afternoon of fight day I received a call from the engineer who was running a test pattern at the Coliseum, advising that we had a problem.

"I don't like the looks of this picture," he said.

"What's wrong with it?" I asked.

"It's awfully dark and I'm concerned about the projector we're using."

Rick and I rushed over to the Coliseum. We didn't like the looks of the picture either, mainly because we didn't have one.

The company promoting the fight always issues instructions on what to do in case of an emergency. We called them immediately and told them we needed another machine. They promised to call back.

In the meantime, we located another projector in Portland which was owned by Theatre Network Television. I reached the local representative and explained my problem. He came down to our office and said, "I could loan you that machine, but if I ever got caught, it would mean my job."

"We can't ask you to do that," I replied. He suggested we get in touch with is office in New York. I reached a fellow at TNT headquarters and explained my problem.

"We offered Teleprompter the use of all of our machines for this show," he said. "They rejected it and we're not going to loan them out piecemeal."

"The fans don't know the difference between Teleprompter and TNT," I told him. "If we have to cancel this show and refund the money, the next several shows will be disasters and you might be promoting one of them."

He promised to get back to me within an hour and, when he did, he flatly rejected the loan of TNT equipment.

Meanwhile, Teleprompter called and said they had located a spare picture tube in San Francisco and promised to put it on the first available flight leaving there at 4 p.m. That meant it would arrive in Portland about 5:30 and the show was scheduled to start at 6:30.

I reached a friend in the Sheriff's office, Ard Pratt, and explained the problem.

"Ard," I said, "please pick that machine up as soon as it arrives at the airport."

He said he would rush it to the Coliseum.

"Ard," I said, "I don't mean wait for it at the baggage department. We instructed them to give that tube to the pilot. I want you to meet that plane on the runway, grab the package from him and come down to the Coliseum with sirens blasting."

He promised he would.

We went to the Coliseum and sweated and waited. The tube's flight arrived and Ard rushed it to the Coliseum, arriving there a little after 6 p.m. The engineer hastily changed the tube and we had some kind of a picture, although not a very good one.

Then about five minutes before the start of the show, a guy tapped me on the shoulder to tell me he was from the Internal Revenue Service.

"We're impounding the gate receipts for this fight," he said.

I didn't know what it was all about, but fortunately most of the money was in the bank and not upstairs in the box office. It turned out that Patterson had signed for a guarantee of one million dollars, payable over a period of twenty years at $50,000 a year. The only problem with this arrangement was that his manager insisted that the money be placed in escrow; the government was contending that this was a "constructive receipt" and Patterson would have to pay taxes on the full amount. Uncle Sam wanted to make sure he was going to collect his money. The IRS guy followed me wherever I went, including a hasty trip to the bathroom.

To make a bad situation worse, our lousy picture showed an even lousier fight. Liston stopped Patterson in the first round. I thought the fans were going to burn the building down.

Rick and I rushed into our old hockey stick room and locked ourselves in until the crowd dispersed; we then emerged with our lives intact. I wouldn't go through a day like it again for a million dollars.

The second occasion on which I feel I let the fans down was when I promoted an NFL pre-season game between the L.A. Rams and the Dallas Cowboys in 1964. The Rams had Terry Baker as a quarterback.

Terry is the most popular sports hero ever produced in Oregon. He was a prep sensation at Jefferson High and led its football team to two state championships. He was also an All-City basketball player and a good baseball player. He went to Oregon State on a basketball scholarship, but decided to turn out for football before his sophomore year. Terry had great success at Oregon State and won the Heisman Trophy his senior year. Needless to say, I was very pleased when Baker signed with the Rams because he would be a tremendous attraction for one of our pre-season games.

I called Dan Reeves on a matter involving hockey a week before the Rams-Cowboy game.

"It's really a coincidence you should call at this time," said Dan. "I have Harlan Svare in the office and I have made a firm request that he play Terry Baker for at least one quarter in our game in Portland next Saturday."

"That will be fine," I told Dan. "Please call me Monday to confirm it so I can publicize it. Baker will help us draw a terrific gate."

That very night, Roman Gabriel, the Rams regular quarterback, was injured in a game against Philadelphia and Terry replaced him. Their other quarterback, Bill Munson, was also hurt so it looked as if the quarterback assignment the following Saturday in Portland would go to Terry and he would play the entire game.

When Jack Teele, the Rams Publicity Director, arrived in Portland Monday, he confirmed that Terry would play the entire game. We publicized Baker's role extensively and attracted a crowd of more than 30,000. The crowd, well beyond capacity, filled all the seats and spilled over into every vantage point around the stadium. Terry started the game and, in the first quarter, guided the Rams to a pair of field goals, although two other scoring drives were halted by fumbles. He did a commendable job.

Then at the start of the second quarter, without advance notice of any kind, Svare inserted Bill Munson, who was supposed to be injured, and kept him there for the remainder of the game. I have never heard such a chorus of boos at a sports event. It continued without interruption throughout the entire game. When it was over, I turned to Teele and said, "Please thank Svare for me for putting me out of business."

If Svare had been honest and announced he was going to play both Baker and Munson, the fans would have had no reason to be upset. But when it had been announced in advance that Baker would play the entire game, to yard him out of there after he had done a creditable job in the first quarter, was the most disgraceful thing with which I have ever been involved.

Dan Reeves called the following Monday and apologized. I answered a couple hundred of letters from fans who rightfully complained about our lack of candor.

I have never wished to see any coach fired, but when Svare was bounced a couple of years later, I heard the news in a saloon. I must confess, I bought a round of drinks for the house.

In recent months, to my great amusement, Ralph Nader has added sports to his consumer movement. Sports fans do not need Nader or any other organization. The fans have the most effective way of telling you they don't like what you're doing. They simply stay away from the ticket tills. A promoter who doesn't hear their message has to be totally deaf and dumb.

Some critics mistakenly contend that winning is the only thing that will draw good crowds. I will be the first to tell you it is better to win than to lose, but as I have learned over the years that winning is not the whole story. If you're respectable, if you're a contender and if you do a good job of promoting, most fans will support you.

Some fans can be a little unreasonable, though. I recall a hockey game in our early games which we lost to Vancouver by a score of 2-1. It was one of the greatest hockey games I have ever seen. The skating was end-to-end, the hitting was clean but effective and the goal tending was sensational. It just so happened that we finished on the wrong end of the score. As I was leaving the building, I ran into a fan who told me in a loud voice—and outraged fans are never soft-spoken—"If that's the way they're going to play, I'll never come back again."

A week later we played the Los Angeles Blades and beat them 13-7. It was one of the most disgraceful games I have ever seen. In hockey, when a team is leading by a score of 3 or 4 to nothing, the players will work hard to preserve a shutout for the goalkeeper. But once the opposition scores, it's to hell with the goalkeeper—every player tries to fatten his scoring records for next year's contract negotiating purposes. That's what happened in this game and it was a terrible performance.

As I was leaving the building, I happened to run into the same fan, who promptly announced, "Now that's more like it—that's the kind of hockey I can support."

You can't win 'em all.

When I invite fans to attend a game I'm promoting, I think they're entitled to the following considerations:

1. There should be a method of purchasing tickets in advance by mail order, and convenient box offices when tickets go on public sale.

2. All tickets must be sold on a first-come first-served basis. The minute someone finds out you're hiding some tickets in your drawer for your friends, you're in trouble. And I can truthfully say, we have never made it a policy to do so. George Rickles, who happens to enjoy Scotch, has turned down cases of the stuff when they were offered in exchange for a couple of playoff tickets. We just simply won't do it. The computer assigns season tickets in the order in which they are purchased.

3. A convenient place to park an automobile should be available.

4. A courteous and efficient gateman should direct the fan to the area of the building in which his seat is located.
5. A friendly and courteous usher should show the fan to his seat.
6. Good security must be provided to protect the majority of the well-behaved fans from the few who spoil it for everyone else.
7. The first-aid room should be well-staffed in case of emergency.
8. Restrooms should be spotless.
9. Well-stocked and efficient concessions should be operating.

To get the fans into our building, we try to do a good job of promotion. This obviously involves good relations with the media. Over the years, I have been treated more than fairly by all of the media in the Portland area. One reason for this is that we have always been honest and forthright with the press. I have found that they will be on your side if you tell them the truth, but if you try to lie to them, they'll mark you lousy forever.

I believe in making it as easy as possible for them to cover our games by furnishing statistical information and background notes to assist them in writing their stories. The trend lately in media coverage is toward background stories and post-game interviews with the players and coaches; we try to make this as quick and convenient as possible for them, because we recognize they have deadlines to meet, especially after night games.

If you're confident you have a good attraction—and I think NBA basketball is the best attraction in professional sports today—then I'm a great believer in exposing the game to as many fans as possible. We do this through our local television contract in which we show a good number of our road games on television, in addition to the games which we aired during the season by the league's contract with the CBS network.

In addition to that, I'm a great believer in such promotions as two-for-one's and discount tickets through arrangements with grocery chains and other radio and television sponsors. It is my belief that once you get the fans into your building and they see your attraction, they may come back another time and buy a ticket at full price. This type of promotion has been very successful for the Trail Blazers. We are currently selling out our building for every game.

The greatest thing we have going to promote interest in professional sports is the playoff system. This arrangement was originally devised by professional hockey. When I first promoted hockey, I knocked the playoff system. Like some fans and members of the media, I couldn't understand why a whole season was played only to eliminate two teams from the playoffs. But I was soon convinced otherwise. There were a couple of years when the Buckaroos had obviously won the league championship by Christmas, but interest in the playoffs made it possible for other teams to draw fans during the remainder of the season. Striving to qualify for the playoffs makes for better games and better entertainment for the fans.

Playoffs proved so effective a system that the National Football League now places eight teams in the playoffs and is considering adding two more. Baseball now uses playoffs prior to the World Series and is also considering adding more teams. It's the most effective way I know to create and maintain interest in a pennant race throughout the entire season. Today the only people I hear knocking the playoffs are old baseball writers who think other professional sports are infringing on baseball coverage. But the fans love it and their votes count.

The most useless commodity in the world is an unsold ticket to a sports event. It costs you money to own unsold tickets— you have to rent space to store them, pay people to count them, pay to shred them and then hual them to a garbage dump at the end of the season.

In discussing the responsibilities of promoters, it should also be pointed out that there are obligations on the part of fans as well. Indeed, fan behavior is rapidly becoming one of the most serious problems we face in the operation of our business.

I have never booed at a sports event. I have used a few choice expletives to label an official, but I have never booed and I deplore the trend toward this kind of behavior which I see among sports audiences all over the country.

Although we don't like the booing, as pros we're prepared to accept it. What really blows my mind is when I hear some stupid adult boo a 12-year old kid who commits an error in a Little League baseball game.

Some fans create more serious disruptions than voicing their displeasure over an official's call. When they start heading for the floor or try to block his way to the dressing room, the only thing to do is give 'em their money back and throw 'em out of the building.

When I watched a game on television and saw a fan throw a whiskey bottle that actually hit an official, I got sick. This type of behavior cannot be tolerated and it's a problem we are starting to come to grips with. The NBA has a Security Department and our Coliseum recently hired a full-time Security Director in an effort to keep the problem under control. It may be that one of the remedies will be to stop selling alcoholic beverages in our buildings. I have never understood the necessity of getting plastered to enjoy a ball game.

I have little patience with old-time "jocks" and sports fans who are constantly talking about the "good old days." The truth is the good old days are right now. Athletes today are bigger, stronger, smarter and better than they were 25 years ago or even 10 years ago. And they will become bigger, stronger, smarter and better with each succeeding athletic generation.

There are many reasons for this, one not much more important than another. Coaching techniques improve each year. Equipment gets better each year. Playing facilities constantly improve. Athletes have better diets. Concentration on weight lifting and conditioning programs improve strength and techniques, and the programs are just in their infancy.

Somewhere there's a kid who will eclipse all of O.J. Simpson's rushing records. Somewhere in the Canadian Prairies there's a kid skating on an outdoor pond who will be a better hockey player than Bobby Orr, the best one I've ever seen. Somewhere there's a kid shooting baskets against a hoop on a garage who will make me forget Jerry West, whom I rate the best I've ever seen. (Bill Walton could do it among the present group of players in the NBA, but it's still a little too early to tell.) Somewhere there's a kid whose ability and exuberance for playing the game will dim the memory of Willie Mays, the best baseball player I ever watched.

Sports fans will be treated to incredible performances in the future. When I was growing up, the four-minute mile was considered *"the"* unbreakable barrier. Today, it's routine.

We will see the day—in the not too distant future—when there will be more international competition. I think that in my lifetime there will be a playoff for the World Basketball Championship and the World Hockey Championship, and a World Series between the United States and Japan.

We will continue to fill stadiums and be entertained on the tube. I envy the fans who will watch these magnificent performances—and I hope I'm still around to hustle 'em some tickets.

Occasionally patience and hard work overcome the inevitable adversities and you get lucky. You can even wind up with a phenomenon such as Blazermania.

This is the ultimate in professional sports and in hustling the tickets—an honest and sincere love affair between a team and its fans.

Blazermania made it all worthwhile.